48 Hours of
KRISTALLNACHT

Also by Mitchell G. Bard, Ph.D.

Will Israel Survive?

1001 Facts Everyone Should Know About Israel
[with Moshe Schwartz]

The Water's Edge and Beyond: Defining the Limits to Domestic
Influence on U.S. Middle East Policy

Myths and Facts: A Guide to the Arab-Israeli Conflict

Forgotten Victims: The Abandonment of Americans
in Hitler's Camps

The Complete Idiot's Guide to World War II

The Complete Idiot's Guide to Middle East Conflict

The Complete History of the Holocaust

The Holocaust (Turning Points in World History)

The Nuremberg Trials (At Issue in History)

The Nuremberg Trials (Eyewitness to History)

From Tragedy to Triumph: The Politics behind
the Rescue of Ethiopian Jewry

The Complete Idiot's Guide to Understanding the Brain

Partners for Change: How U.S.-Israel Cooperation Can Benefit
America

U.S.-Israel Relations: Looking to the Year 2000

Building Bridges: Lessons for America from Novel Israeli Approaches
to Promote Coexistence

The Founding of the State of Israel

48 Hours of
KRISTALLNACHT

Night of Destruction/Dawn of the Holocaust

An Oral History

MITCHELL G. BARD, Ph.D.

THE LYONS PRESS
Guilford, Connecticut

An Imprint of The Globe Pequot Press

The Lyons Press in an imprint of The Globe Pequot Press.

Cover design by Jane Sheppard
Text design by Sheryl P. Kober

Library of Congress Cataloging-in-Publication Data

Bard, Mitchell Geoffrey, 1959–
    48 hours of Kristallnacht: night of destruction/dawn of the Holocaust: an oral
history/Mitchell G. Bard.
        p. cm.
    Includes bibliographical references and index.
    ISBN 978-1-59921-445-0
    1. Jews—Persecutions—Germany. 2. Kristallnacht, 1938.
3. Jews—Germany—History—1933–1945. I Title.
    DS134.255.B37 2008
    940.53'1842—dc22

                                                          2008024727

Printed in the United States of America

10 9 8 7 6 5 4 3 2 1

This book is dedicated to the memory of those who lived and died during Kristallnacht and all that came after. It is also dedicated to all those who fight today to ensure that the events of that night are remembered so they may never be repeated.

Contents

Contents

Acknowledgments

I would like to thank the survivors who took the time to tell their often painful stories, and the writers and interviewers who documented their eyewitness accounts.

I gratefully acknowledge the USC Shoah Foundation Institute for Visual History and Education, University of Southern California, for allowing us to use many powerful testimonies (see Appendix F for the complete list) that have helped me to convey the impact of Kristallnacht on the lives of individuals and families.

I would like to thank Tom Holloway for permission to use Susan's story from his Timewitnesses Web site, haGalil.com for permission to use the memoir by Ernest Günter Fontheim, Selden Smith and the South Carolina Council on the Holocaust for permission to use the accounts of Martha Bauer and Peter Becker, and the Klein Foundation and family for permission to quote Kurt Klein's testimony. I also want to thank Shulamith (Sophie) Yaari-Nussbaum for permission to quote her story, which appears in Ellen Land-Weber's book, *To Save a Life: Stories of Holocaust Rescue*.

I am also grateful to Yad Vashem for its full-time commitment to documenting the Holocaust and its generosity in sharing material.

The same can be said of the U.S. Holocaust Memorial Museum. In particular I would like to thank the museum for permission to use interviews with Carola Steinhardt, Anna Bluethe, Jacob Wiener, Gad Beck, Kurt Ladner, and Armin Kern, as well as the text from "The United States and the Refugee Crisis" from the museum's Web site. I want to especially thank Michlean Amir for her assistance in navigating the archives and providing materials for the book.

Acknowledgments

I want to thank Gary Krebs for approaching me to pursue this important and fascinating project, and Keith Wallman for his work in editing the book. I also want to thank Ellen Urban for overseeing the project and Rose Marye Boudreaux for copyediting the manuscript.

Finally, I want to thank my research assistants, Jonathan Lord and Allison Krant, without whom this project could not have been completed and whose comments and suggestions improved the manuscript along the way.

Introduction

Imagine you are nine years old, sleeping soundly in your warm bed. Before going to sleep you went through the normal bedtime ritual of brushing your teeth and washing your hands and face. Your mother came in to read a story. When you wake up, you'll eat breakfast and then go to school like you do every day.

You're suddenly awakened by loud banging coming from the front door. You're not fully awake yet, but then you hear the door crash to the ground and people running in. As you bolt upright, your mother rushes in and grabs you by the hand. She leads you downstairs to the living room where you see your father shouting at a group of men who are all dressed in brown shirts and carrying axes and knives and broom handles.

One of the men hits your father with the end of a knife across the forehead, and he begins to bleed. "Daddy!" you shout, and rush to his side.

The other men begin to smash the tables and chairs and rip the upholstery of the couch. The hoodlums break the windows facing the street and begin to pull the family's books from the shelves and throw them out the window. You can hear the sound of dishes breaking in the kitchen as another intruder pulls everything from the cabinets and throws it on the ground.

The man who hit your father says, "You're under arrest. Come with me!"

"Why are you taking him? He hasn't done anything wrong," you cry as you rush over and cling to his leg.

Now the man comes toward you and grabs you by the arm and roughly throws you to the ground. Before you can move, you see your father being pulled out the door and pushed down the stairs; he trips and rolls to the bottom. The other men follow, pausing only to throw a glass lamp onto the floor where it shatters.

Your mother rushes out the door and down the steps, shouting after the men dragging away your father, "Where are you taking him?"

You reach her side in time to hear the response, "Check with the Gestapo."

Your mother begins to cry, and she bends down to hug you. Over her shoulder you can see smoke rising from the synagogue burning down the street. The store windows of the Jewish businesses nearby are all broken, and people are walking out of the stores with clothes, jewelry, and groceries. People are shouting and laughing amid the sound of glass shattering.

It is a night you will never forget. Later, people will call it Kristallnacht.

On November 9 and 10, 1938, rampaging mobs throughout Germany and the newly acquired territories of Austria and the Sudetenland freely attacked Jews in the street, in their homes, and at their places of work and worship. At least 96 Jews were killed (Read and Fisher say the number was at least 236, including 43 women and 13 children[1]) and hundreds more injured, more than 1,300 synagogues were burned (and possibly as many as 2,000), almost 7,500 Jewish businesses were destroyed, and countless cemeteries and schools were vandalized. No estimates were available, but untold amounts of precious commodities, such as art-works, were lost as hooligans destroyed whatever they saw without regard for its value.

A total of 30,000 Jews were arrested and sent to concentration camps on those days. At least 4,600 Viennese Jews were sent to Dachau. About 2,500 Jews were arrested in Hamburg and transported to Oranienburg. Another 2,621 Jews from Frankfurt were sent to Buchenwald. The average period of imprisonment was four to six weeks for older men and longer for some of the younger Jews.[2] More than 5,000 people died in Buchenwald, Sachsenhausen, and Dachau in the aftermath of the pogroms.[3] Tens of thousands more German and Austrian Jews would die in the camps during the war.

The Germans initially referred to the 48 hours of mayhem as the "Jew Action." No one is sure when it originated, but the term "Crystal Night" or Kristallnacht (or, less commonly, Reichskristallnacht) eventually came to be the term associated with the pogroms of November 9–10, 1938, because of the widespread destruction of windows that left shattered glass strewn throughout the streets. Many Jews and scholars, however, find the term offensive and object to its use. As Walter Pehle wrote, "It is clear that the term Crystal Night serves to foster a vicious minimalizing of its memory, a discounting of grave reality: such cynical appellations function to reinterpret manslaughter and murder, arson and robbery, plunder, and massive property damage, transforming these into a glistening event marked by sparkle and gleam."[4]

On the 40th anniversary of Kristallnacht, Helmut Schmidt, the former West German chancellor, spoke in the synagogue in Cologne about the significance of those 48 hours:

The German night, whose observance after the passage of forty years has brought us together today, remains a cause of bitterness and shame. In those places where the houses of God stood in flames, where a signal from those in power set off a train of destruction and robbery, of humiliation, abduction and incarceration— there was an end to peace, to justice, to humanity. The night of 9 November 1938 marked one of the stages along the path leading down to hell.[5]

CHAPTER 1

Warning Signs

Germany was one of Europe's most cultured, sophisticated soci-
eties, and all German Jews considered themselves integral to
that society. Though a tiny minority of the country—about 525,000
people, or less than 1 percent of the population—they were among
the elite of German society: prominent doctors, lawyers, professors,
and industrialists. Many were assimilated and were not practicing
Jews; some had even converted. In the racial ideology of Adolf Hitler, however, German Jews' self-identification was irrelevant. For
Hitler, Jews were parasites whose diseased nature came from their
blood, so their religious beliefs and practices made no difference;
it was the impurity of Jewish blood that threatened the racial purity
and superiority of the Aryan race.

The official persecution of the Jews began in April 1933, when
the Nazis initiated a boycott of Jewish businesses throughout Germany. Signs and graffiti warned Germans not to buy from the Jews.
This boycott was followed by the enactment of a law barring Jews
from civil service jobs, including positions as teachers in schools
and universities. Two years later, German Jews were stripped of their
citizenship and barred from marrying Aryans. Because some of the
new laws were announced at a Nazi rally at Nuremberg, they became
known as the Nuremberg Laws. These were just some of the 400

separate pieces of legislation that were adopted between the time Hitler came to power and World War II began that prevented Jews from working, going to school, or otherwise taking part in German society. These decrees robbed them of their possessions and demonized their religion. Many Jews believed the discriminatory measures would cease after the enactment of the Nuremberg Laws in 1935, and they would have to accept life as second-class citizens, and most were prepared to do so.

The situation actually improved briefly as Hitler focused on putting Germany's best foot forward in advance of the 1936 Berlin Olympics. Before, during, and for a short time afterward, the Nazis displayed their nationalistic spirit in a way that reinforced the positive image of Germans. Shortly thereafter, however, the situation for Jews began to deteriorate further. They were prevented from staying in hotels; going to restaurants, theaters, or shops; or even sitting on park benches designated for Aryans. By the middle of 1938, most Jewish businesses had been taken over by the Germans.

In March 1938, Germany annexed Austria, and 183,000 more Jews became subject to the Nazis' discriminatory policies. Still, many Jews simply could not conceive of anything permanently altering their status, let alone conceive of the dimensions of Hitler's ultimate plan. It was this disbelief, even as the persecution against them went from bad to worse, that led so many to stay in their homes rather than flee. By the time those who remained realized what Hitler intended—and the willingness of their fellow Germans to go along—it was too late to escape.

The world also had a different image of Germany than the Jews who lived inside the country. On September 29, 1938, France and

Britain had negotiated an agreement recognizing Hitler's annexation of the Sudetenland region of Czechoslovakia. British Prime Minister Neville Chamberlain announced after the Munich Agreement that it would lead to "peace for our time."

✡ No Crime to Be Jewish ✡

The progressive steps to remove the Jews from German society still allowed them to remain in their homes, and most still enjoyed a certain degree of comfort. The most serious indication that Jews were no longer welcome in Germany occurred on October 27, 1938, when about 18,000 Jews from around the Reich were arrested and transported by train to the Polish border. They were allowed to take only one suitcase with them, and all of the rest of their possessions were either looted by their neighbors or seized by the Nazis. Only 4,000 were allowed into Poland; the rest were stranded at the border.

The expulsion of the Polish Jews ultimately had an unexpected and even more devastating impact on those who remained in Germany.

Among the Jews sent to Poland was the Grynszpan family. They had been expelled from Hanover where they had lived for the previous 27 years. Their oldest son, 17-year-old Herschel, escaped the deportation because he was living in Paris, where he had moved two years earlier to find work. Herschel received a postcard from his sister Berta describing how the family had been arrested and sent by cattle car at night without food or water to the Polish border. Once they reached the frontier, the Nazi SS guards forced the Jews to run, whipping those who were not obedient or quick enough to escape the lash. Inside Poland, the Jews were housed in filthy horse stables. The starving people eventually received a shipment of bread, but not enough arrived to feed everyone.

The postcard infuriated Herschel. He decided to seek revenge for the treatment of his family.

At 8:35 a.m. on November 6, Herschel went to a sporting and hunting goods store in Paris and bought a gun. About an hour later he calmly presented himself at the German Embassy and asked to see the ambassador, Johannes von Welczeck. The ambassador was actually heading out and overheard the request, but ignored it and continued on his way. Herschel insisted on seeing someone to whom he could deliver what he claimed was an important document. His persistence led him to Third Secretary Ernst vom Rath.

Ironically, vom Rath was under investigation by the Gestapo because he was suspected of lacking the proper zealotry expected of a Nazi official, particularly toward the Jews.[6] Grynszpan knew nothing about the man except that he represented the government that had deported and abused his family. When vom Rath asked to see the document he was carrying, Herschel shouted, "You are a *sale boche* [filthy kraut] and here, in the name of 12,000 persecuted Jews, is your document!" He then fired five shots at close range; the first two penetrated the diplomat's stomach, the rest missed. Vom Rath was wounded but still conscious. Herschel seemed surprised he wasn't dead and remained standing calmly in the office as the scene grew chaotic. Herschel did not resist when police came and escorted him from the embassy to a nearby police station. "I did it to avenge my parents, who are living in misery in Germany," Her-

4

schel informed the officers.[7] He later told his interrogators, "It's not a crime to be Jewish. I'm not a dog. I have the right to live and the Jewish people has the right to exist in this world. Everywhere I am persecuted like an animal."[8]

Vom Rath was rushed to the hospital after the shooting, but he succumbed to his injuries and died at 5:30 p.m. on November 9.

✡ A Failed Coup ✡

Coincidentally, this was the 15th anniversary of the "Beer Hall Putsch," which Anthony Read and David Fisher call the "holiest day in the entire Nazi calendar."[9] This was the date Hitler first tried to take over Germany and when he first achieved prominence.

In 1921 Adolf Hitler became chairman of what was then called the National Socialist German Workers' Party (Nationalsozialistische Deutsche Arbeiterpartei, or NSDAP) and later became known as the Nazi Party. He created his own personal army of storm troopers, the Sturmabteilung, or SA. The group wore brown uniforms and was subsequently referred to as "Brownshirts." They also had their own marching song, named after the Berlin leader of the SA, Horst Wessel, who, according to Nazi legend, was murdered by a communist in 1930.

The German economy was in distress in the early 1920s, and the German currency had collapsed by 1923. Hitler saw the public's discontent as his opportunity to seize power. On November 8 he led his "army" to a beer hall in Bavaria where local government leaders were holding a meeting. The Nazis quickly captured the politicians, and Hitler put himself in charge of a new national government. The group then marched on the former Bavarian War Ministry building when the police opened fire. The man beside Hitler was killed as he pulled his leader to the ground, and the Nazis all fled.

Hitler was arrested and sentenced to five years in prison. It was during his incarceration that he wrote *Mein Kampf* (My Struggle), which laid out his views on the centrality of Aryan purity to historical progress, the mortal danger posed by world Jewry and international communism, the necessity of rebuilding German power, and the importance of expanding Germany's borders to provide the living space—Lebensraum—the German people required.

Hitler was released from prison after only nine months and began a tradition of giving an emotional speech on the anniversary of the revolt. After he came to power, these events became grand festivals that transformed the failed putsch into tributes to mythical fallen heroes.

✡ Goebbels Seizes the Opportunity ✡

The news that vom Rath was fighting for his life in a Paris hospital came in the midst of the 1938 gathering of the party faithful to commemorate the Beer Hall Putsch. Hitler's minister of propaganda, Joseph Goebbels, saw the killing as an opportunity to take the persecution of the Jews to a new level. It also was a chance for him to try to redeem himself in Hitler's eyes, as the Führer had criticized the effectiveness of his propaganda and had also recently learned that the propaganda minister was having a scandalous affair with a Czech actress.

After the shooting, Goebbels ordered all newspaper editors in the Reich to print on page one reports about the attack on vom Rath by a Jew. The Nazi Party newspaper, *Völkischer Beobachter,* set the tone with the November 8 headline: "Jewish Murder Attempt in Paris—Member of the German Embassy Critically Wounded by Shots—The Murdering Knave a 17-Year-Old Jew." The text of the editorial accompanying the article made clear all Jews were to blame for the attack in Paris, and much more. "It is clear what conclusions the German people will draw from this latest event. We shall no longer tolerate a situation where hundreds of thousands of Jews within our territory control entire streets of shops, throng places of public entertainment, and pocket the wealth of German leaseholders as 'foreign' landlords while their racial brothers incite war against Germany and shoot down German officials...."[10]

The following day, the Nazi paper's headline screamed, "The Shots in Paris Will Not Go Unpunished!" and Goebbels's paper, *Der Angriff,* proclaimed, "From this vile deed arises the imperative demand for immediate action against the Jews, with the most severe consequences."[11]

The German media was filled with such reports because the propaganda ministry gave instructions on how to cover the shooting of vom Rath: "All German newspapers must carry large-scale reportage on the assassination attempt against the life of the third secretary in the German Embassy in Paris. The news must completely dominate page 1. News reports on the grave condition of Mr. vom Rath will be issued by the DNB. His condition is extremely serious. It should be pointed out in several editorials that this assassination attempt perpetrated by a Jew must have the most serious consequences for Jews in Germany, even for the foreign Jews in Germany."[12]

There was no response from the Jewish press because all the newspapers had already been closed by the Nazis. On November 8, the screws were tightened further when an edict also banned Jews from attending Aryan elementary schools.

On November 9 Hitler sat down for the gala feast at Munich's Old Town Hall to relive the glorious revolution of 1923. Just before 9:00 p.m., he was informed that vom Rath had died. He and Goebbels had a quiet exchange. In his diary, Goebbels said Hitler had told him to allow demonstrations against Jewish homes and businesses to continue. "The police should be withdrawn. For once the Jews should get the feel of popular anger." Goebbels said he immediately gave instructions to the party and the police.[13]

One might have expected Hitler to exploit the situation and deliver a fiery address denouncing the Jews for the murder. Curiously, however, Hitler said nothing about vom Rath's death and left the hall without making a speech (he also said nothing when he later attended the funeral). Goebbels then seized the opportunity to rouse the party faithful by standing and telling the crowd that a Jew had killed a "loyal servant of the Reich." He said the attack by international Jewry could not go unchallenged. "Our people must be told, and their answer must be ruthless, forthright, salutary! I ask you to listen to me, and together we must plan what is to be our answer to Jewish murder and the threat of international Jewry to our glorious German Reich!"[14]

He recorded in his diary that his remarks were met with "stormy applause. All are instantly at the phones. Now people will act."[15]

✡ Following Orders ✡

Three of Hitler's closest advisors were not present at the Munich celebration. Hermann Göring, his right-hand man, was on a train to Berlin and didn't learn about the demonstrations that took place during the night until the following morning. Heinrich Himmler, the head of the Gestapo and the SS, who later attributed the pogrom to Goebbels's "lust for power," was in Munich, as was the security chief, Reinhard Heydrich, but neither was present at the Old Town Hall for the festivities. Himmler first learned of the plan to attack the Jews at 11:30 p.m. on November 9 at Hitler's apartment. After consulting with Hitler, Himmler sent instructions to Gestapo Chief Heinrich Müller to keep the SS out of the fray but to arrest wealthy Jews and send them to concentration camps.

At 11:55 p.m. on November 9, Müller sent an order to all police offices advising them that "Actions against Jews, especially against their synagogues, will take place throughout the Reich shortly. They are not to be interfered with. . . . Preparations are to be made for the arrest of about 20,000 to 30,000 Jews in the Reich. Above all, well-to-do Jews are to be selected."

His telegram instructed his minions to collect any archival material from the synagogues and said that "the sharpest measures" should be taken if any Jews were found in possession of weapons (another directive said they should be held in custody for 20 years). Müller added that the Gestapo should prevent looting and other illegal activities (see Appendix A).

Later that evening, at 1:20 a.m., Heydrich sent out a more detailed message that instructed the police to arrest healthy Jewish adult males of "not too advanced age" and transport them to concentration camps; to destroy Jewish businesses and homes but not loot them, to ensure that no German lives or property was endangered; to seize documents of historical importance from synagogues and Jewish institutions; and to refrain from harming foreigners even if they were Jews (see Appendix B).[16]

Shortly thereafter, an order was sent from the office of Hitler's deputy, Rudolf Hess, stating that Jewish businesses and houses should not be burned. As Read and Fisher note, the police and the SD (the security service of the SS) were given specific instructions about what they could and could not do, but the SA was left without any official guidance. Three months later, the Supreme Tribunal of the Nazi Party would note: "It was normal practice to give hazy, unspecific instructions for any action which the party did not wish to appear to instigate," so many party members "acquired the habit of overstepping the bounds of their instructions . . . particularly in arranging illegal demonstrations."[17]

Individual branches of the SA also got their own instructions. In Cologne, for example, orders first arrived at 12:45 a.m. on November 10. They instructed members to set fire to all synagogues at 4:00 a.m. At 6:00 a.m. Jewish shops and homes in the city center were to be attacked. By 8:00 a.m. the suburbs were to be targeted. The entire operation was to end at 1:00 p.m. The police were also instructed to supply the SA with weapons along with the addresses of Jewish property to be destroyed.[18]

An indication of the premeditation of the attacks was the preparations made in concentration camps. On November 10 a memo was issued that said, "I advise you that Dachau, Buchenwald, and Sachsenhausen [Oranienburg] concentration camps are each in a position to accommodate ten thousand detainees."[19] Ultimately 30,000 Jews would be imprisoned over the next few days. The police had also begun to disarm Jews and had confiscated more than 1,700 firearms and 20,000 rounds of ammunition in Berlin alone.[20] The forethought of the pogrom was also clear, as some Jews were tipped off by sympathetic Germans about the plan. Ernst Herzfeld, for example, was told by friends in the evening of November 9 that he should go to Berlin to avoid exposing himself to risk.[21]

The violence actually began even before any formal orders were issued and before vom Rath died. Partly in response to the hysteria whipped up by the German press, Jews were attacked, businesses looted, and synagogues destroyed in Kassel and Magdeburg-Anhalt on November 8. A local paper in Kassel reported, "the smashed windowpanes and damaged interiors of synagogues and other Jewish institutions are the spontaneous price to be paid by world Jewry, a price this people of agitators and swindlers owes to its own actions."[22]

These spasms of violence were limited. The nationwide attacks on the Jews in Germany and Austria began just before midnight on November 9, when demonstrators set fire to a display window of a Jewish textile business in Munich. Three minutes later, the fire department received a call that the first synagogue was on fire. It would not be long before alarms would be sounding throughout the Reich.

CHAPTER 2

A Harsh Childhood

Many of the survivors of Kristallnacht were only children in 1938. The following accounts give a sense of the horror these young Jews experienced as strangers broke into their houses, destroyed their belongings, and often arrested their fathers and other members of the family. The scenes they witnessed would haunt many for their entire lives.

In the German capital of Berlin, the violence did not start until 2:00 a.m., after the police had a chance to "isolate Jewish buildings, cut telephone wires, switch off electricity supplies and heating to Jewish shops and businesses so as to prevent untoward accidents, and to set up road barriers to divert traffic away from the areas where the mobs were to be loose."[23]

✡ Don't Make Any Waves ✡

Later on the morning of November 10, five-year-old Gisela Golombek went to school. "There was a big commotion in the classroom. Teachers came running in and the principal came in—there were all girls, no boys—and he said, 'I want you to get your coats and quietly go home and if you have a way to go along side streets please do that.

Do not stop anywhere. Do not look at anything. Do not congregate. Do not go in groups. At the max, go in two or three people.' In other words, she was saying, 'Don't make any waves.'

"I had no brothers or sisters. I went with two little girls. They were very dear to me. Elie and Sonia Danziger. They were like me, very fair. I think she had golden hair. I think that saved us because no one thought we were Jews. I took us on a roundabout route, and all along the way it appeared to me the city was on fire. Then we passed the big synagogue and it was burning. I couldn't believe my eyes. The city wasn't burning, just Jewish businesses, synagogues, department stores. And people came and ransacked everything, and there was vile language which was splattered all over the buildings. Windows of stores had been knocked down and whatever merchandise had been on the shelves was on the street and people were taking it away. I was in absolute terror. I didn't know what to do. Sonia said 'I think you better come home with us and that's what I did. I went home with them.'

"Mrs. Danziger was stupid. She should have called my mother or left a message. My mother was in absolute terror. She could not find me. She combed the city up and down and down and up. . . . She finally decided to go to my school and ask if someone had seen me leave. Apparently someone told her I had gone with the Danziger girls, so she came over to the house. She looked like something out of a fairy tale. She looked like a dragon, spewing fire, she was in such utter rage; her face was red. And she struck me. I've never forgotten that. She just turned around and struck me with all her might. I didn't cry, I just looked at her in horror and said, 'Why are you hitting me?' She said to me, 'How could you? How could you?' But I said,

'Mommy, I was afraid to go home by myself.' She said, 'Put on your coat and let's go.'

"We never ever spoke of it again. She never apologized. I never asked her to. I never brought it up. I always felt she was wrong, but then later, as an adult, I understood how she felt. I was an only child. She had three or four pregnancies which she never carried through. I was born weighing two and a half pounds. I was a seven-month baby. I meant everything to her. To think she lost me somewhere along the way was more than she could bear and she really fought like a tiger. She really came at me. I didn't know her for the moment. Then we went home and I would have to say all hell broke loose. You didn't dare walk the street. You didn't dare turn on a light. And my mother started to dismantle everything in the house because we had been asked to leave since dirty Jews didn't belong in their society."

Gisela's mother then began to destroy their possessions. A few items she saved to give to people who had worked for the family, such as the person who stoked their fire. "My mother said, 'Gisela I don't want you to be upset. If we can give things to people we love, it makes sense, but you don't give things to your enemies, to people who want to destroy you. And since we can't take it with us, we'll destroy it ourselves.' She said, 'Please don't cry.'

"Everything of my mother's that I ever wanted was always open to me, her records and books. I could read anything I wanted. I loved all these things. Everything was very dear to me. She took hundreds of books and most of them were beautifully done. My father was good at book binding and he bound them in red or black leather. We tore them apart and put them in the oven. When I think about it, it was like Hitler. He destroyed literature. But that's what my mother did. She destroyed everything she couldn't take with her. They had bought me a piano, which was not a new piano, but I had piano lessons. I can still see my mother tearing up the ivories and cutting up the strings and scratching up the beautiful wood with a knife or whatever she had in her hand. She wasn't going to leave it there for them to enjoy. Whatever we couldn't take, she made mayhem out of."[24]

✡ The Longest Tram Ride ✡

Robert Dratwa was a 13-year-old in Berlin on Kristallnacht. "Late in the afternoon it was getting dark and my mother was with two children and was afraid they might come into the house. Across from us was a tram station and she decided to go on the tram. The station was very near a big shop equivalent to Macy's, and they smashed the windows, so she was afraid to walk in the streets so we just rode the tram, changing from one tram to another where we felt safer than in the street. Later there were less people in the street. I remember around dawn going back home."[25]

✡ Two Kids Left, Two Kids Right ✡

Fred Marcus was 14 years old and attended a Jewish high school in Berlin. "I had to take an elevated train to get to school. I met my good friend every day on the train. I threw my briefcase across the car to where Herbert was standing and he looked white as a sheet.

I said, 'What's wrong. Are you sick? Did you have trouble with your parents?' He was very uncommunicative.

"When we got off, he stopped me and said, 'You know when the train goes by Fasanenstrasse, the synagogue was burning and the fire department was there but it looked like they weren't doing very much.'

"As we got to school, every kid who passed the school reported the synagogue had been set on fire. That was the beginning of the end. I don't know if it was that occasion or another that it was deemed too dangerous to keep several hundred Jewish school children in the school building at one time. I remember very distinctly a little door being opened in the main gate and the school director standing by the door. We were divided into those going out to the left and the right and he would send out two kids left, two kids right, and he would look down the street until they had turned the corners before letting the next kids go. They were afraid to let all the kids on the street en masse."[26]

✡ You Don't Look Jewish ✡

Helga Relation said there was a sense of expectation following the attack on vom Rath in Paris. Helga was living in Berlin on Kristallnacht. She was just 14 years old. "The speeches indicated something was going to happen. And this was 1938; things were already bad. My father must have known because we decided to leave the apartment and we went to my grandmother. My mother and my father slept in my grandmother's bedroom and I slept in the bottom of a trundle bed. I don't think that we went home for about five days. It was a horrible night and we could hear the breaking of windows, glass, but we didn't look. We didn't have the lights on. We didn't want any attention onto us in that house. When we got up the next morning we found out that the synagogues had been burned. Glass was all over, all the Jews' stores were broken in to, all the glass was broken. Lots and lots of people had been arrested that night. But again, we were lucky. My father wasn't arrested at that time.

"We had some people living across the street. I didn't know them. I mean, you didn't know the people but I saw the people. I saw the man, I think it was a man, if I remember, it was somebody who was literally thrown out of the window to the street. It was a horrible sight. My parents pulled me away from the window."[27]

✡ It Only Happens to Other People ✡

"On the 10th I had to go to work," Robert Behr recalled. "As I went out of the house, I saw all the stores were smashed and Nazi stormtroopers in their brown uniforms. Police stood around and didn't do anything. Berlin had always been a liberal city. Berliners as a whole have been tolerant to Jews. Suddenly all that changed. Berliners turned out to be no different than anyone else.

"I rode a bicycle to work. We lived near the 5th avenue of Berlin and I found myself terrified. When I got to work I called my mother and told her if she doesn't have to go out of the house, don't go.

"It was a real culture shock for my family. We didn't even know until few days later that my father had been arrested because my parents were divorced and they weren't living together. It was an absolutely frightening experience. All the things that we thought only happened to other people suddenly happened in our town."[28]

✡ Leaving Camp ✡

Kurt Jacoby had turned 10 years old two weeks before Kristallnacht. "I happened to be in a summer camp, in the suburbs of Berlin. It was a very large Jewish camp. We were doing our games and whatever we did there. At noon I vividly remember a car pulling up with four SS men. They asked where our supervisors were. They went into their office and they came out, gathered the children, and said, 'Listen, we have a little problem. We have to close the camp. You'll all have to go back to Berlin. We will notify your parents to pick you up at the station.'

"Of what I remember, these officers were very courteous, not rude at all, and nobody really got scared. I remember my father picking me up on Kristallnacht with a taxi. It was a rainy night and he was telling me about what happened and that he had made up his mind to leave Germany and go to Shanghai. He also told me at that time that he had asked his sister and my mother's sister, which was my aunt, to come along. Both of them thought we were crazy to go to China and they said they weren't going to go. So we left, and they stayed."[29]

✡ Orphans Again ✡

Dinslaken is an industrial city in North Rhine-Westphalia, Germany. Today, it is known for its harness horse race track. At 9:30 a.m. on

November 10, the bell began to ring at the Dinslaken Orphanage. When the director of the orphanage opened the door, 50 men stormed into the building and rushed into the empty dining room and began to break tables and chairs. The commotion frightened the children who had been told to gather in the study hall. As the sounds of destruction reverberated through the house, the children became more agitated, and the director ordered them out into the street, hoping that they would find safety in a more public place.

"Obediently, the children raced down a back staircase out the door wearing whatever they had on, most inadequately dressed for the cold, damp November weather. The director and the children rushed toward the town hall and found a group of policemen who they looked to for help. Instead, one of the officers shouted: 'Jews do not get protection from us! Vacate the area together with your children as quickly as possible!' The policeman then forced the director and his charges back to the orphanage. When the director was unable to produce a key quickly enough to open the back gate, the policeman took out his bayonet and forced the door open.

"Imagining the worst, the director told the officer, 'The best thing is to kill me and the children, then our ordeal will be over quickly!' The policeman laughed and ordered him to stay in the orphanage.

"From the garden, the children watched as the men inside the orphanage tore apart everything they could find—books, chairs, beds, tables, linens—and threw them through holes in the wall where they had already pulled out windows and doors. The police stood by watching the destruction while a mob of spectators gathered, many of whom had been regular visitors or suppliers to the orphanage. No one spoke out against the violence.

"Less than an hour passed before the sounds of sirens could be heard in the town. The director looked up in the sky and saw smoke. It was coming from the direction of the synagogue. Thankfully, he thought the fire department was on the way to put out the blaze. Later he learned, however, that the fire fighters had not been sent to save the synagogue or the Jewish homes nearby that had also been torched. Their mission was to ensure the houses of non-Jews would not be caught in the conflagration."[30]

Dinslaken was not the only orphanage to be targeted by the roaming gangs of Nazis. In Esslingen, in the Stuttgart region of Germany, Ina Rothschild wrote that "between noon and 1 o'clock, civilians and SA men armed with axes and heavy hammers appeared in the dining room of the orphanage and forced us, shouting 'Get out of here!' to leave the building and gather at the compost heap in back. Some of the children ran away, the rest were guarded together by the SA. . . . While some men did nothing . . . the others proceeded to destroy everything within reach. Books were tossed from the rooms of the teachers and from our apartment; prayer books, Torah scrolls, and memorial plaques were thrown from the prayer hall, and all this was placed on a bonfire. One of these ruffians threatened that the children who were crying would also be tossed on the pile and burned." Ultimately, the children were allowed to go away with friends and other acquaintances.[31]

✡ But Mommy, We Are Not Jewish ✡

Sophie Nussbaum was 13 years old. She lived in Emden, a city and seaport in northwest Germany on the River Ems. Her father owned a small grocery shop. On November 9, she was awakened from a sound sleep by knocking at the door.

"'Open up! We're taking all of you to Palestine,' they shouted.

"We never believed that, of course. They broke our windowpanes, and the house became very cold. Quickly, my mother tried to gather up some valuables—some gold things—but one of the men hit her on the arm with his gun, making her drop them. They made us leave everything behind when they took us away—to a Christian school. We were standing there, outside in the cold, still in our night clothes, with only a coat thrown over. They kept bringing more and more Jewish people from all over the neighborhood. Babies were crying.

"The horse butcher and his family were there. He was Jewish, but his wife was not, and they had not raised their children as Jews. I can still hear the daughter crying, 'But Mommy, we are not Jewish!'

"'You are not here because of your religion, but because of your blood!' said the SS.

"Then they made everyone lie face down on the ground. It was quite cold.

"'Now, they will shoot us,' we thought. We were very afraid.

"Then abruptly, 'Get up!'

"They kept us there until the sky was light, and then they took us into the gymnasium, and called out everyone's name. They had lists—wonderfully organized. After that, we were allowed to go home. But they kept the men.

"When we got home, we found an SS man with a gun walking up and down our street. Everything was smashed up, but we were not allowed to go into our shop—it was forbidden. He said that it wasn't ours any longer, that we owned nothing, we were nothing, our lives were nothing. When the SS got to the furthest corner, I ran inside and took out what I could.

"My mother was afraid they might come back to our house that night, so she sent my younger sister Ruth and me to sleep at our Aunt Lena's house—somehow they had forgotten about Aunt Lena. My mother and grandmother, who was living with us, went upstairs to the flat above ours, to stay with Mrs. Ludenstein. About 4 o'clock in the morning they heard heavy footsteps, then nothing—everything was quiet. My mother was afraid to go down, but my grandmother said, 'I'll go.' She found my father sitting there, making himself a cup of coffee.

"The SS had sent father home because he had influential Christian friends who had interceded on his behalf. The other men were not so lucky. When Ruth and I came back the next morning, we overheard the street cleaners saying, 'Oh, during the night they brought all the Jewish men to the train station, and took them away.' They sent them to Sachsenhausen and Oranienburg concentration camps.

"But my father was free, and we were so happy. We cleaned up the mess, and they let us open the shop."[32]

✡ Bluffing the Perpetrators ✡

"When Kristallnacht came, we already knew what to expect," recalled Leo Rechter. He was 11 years old when the hoodlums came and burned the synagogue in Vienna, Austria. "We saw the fire. The sky was red. When you looked out the window you saw the sky was red all over Vienna. My mother and my younger sister were hiding somewhere, I don't know where. My father and I stayed in the apartment. And they came around. The SA, a group of five, six people in black boots and brown shirts and they asked the super, a Polish guy, to tell them all the apartment numbers where Jews live. And sure enough he was delighted to give out the numbers. So they came and they knocked on the door and my father opened it. And they grabbed him right away by the throat and they pushed him against the wall." The person who appeared to be the leader then entered. He recognized Leo. Apparently he had tutored him and immediately told the others, "Let's leave this one alone." The group then left.

About a half hour later, the Rechters heard another knock on the door, and two SA men pushed their way inside. "They said, 'Are you Jewish?' They started yelling at my father. And this time my father bluffed them. He started yelling at them, 'What's the matter with you people? That's the second time you're coming around over here! Have you no shame? And why don't you get lost? You already were here! Now you're disturbing my day!' And he managed to bluff them, after all, they were not too bright. And they left."[33]

✡ I Just Couldn't Understand It ✡

Dennis Urstein recalled Kristallnacht in Vienna as a 14-year-old. "First, they burned down the synagogue, and all the other synagogues. Then people were put on the street, cleaning the streets with toothbrushes and being spit upon and hit upon, and 'zal jude' this and 'zal jude' that. My mother was shaking in her boots. She didn't want anybody to go out. I went out. I didn't know better, and nothing happened to me, thank God. I just couldn't understand it. I couldn't understand why it was done."[34]

✡ Nothing But a Pincushion ✡

Edmund Rosenblum was 18 and worked in the family store in Vienna. "Our store was still open, it was not open for business; it was just there. We worked sort of behind closed doors, my father, myself, and my mother. And they came with a truck. The corner building was an electrical supply house. They ripped that open. The one next to it was a grocery store. They took out whatever little food they had because there was not much food left for Jewish people in Vienna. All the food was delegated to go to the army. And they got through with that, they cleaned out whatever they had in there, bags of beans and peas, no fresh food of any kind. Then they came to us.

"There was sort of an iron grate and they ripped it open. My mother and myself came downstairs, we opened the door and they came in. There was one man, an SS man in charge, with a black uniform, but the others were brownshirt men, SAs. And, being a clothing store, we had some ready-made clothing and some for fitting and some pants and coats and sport jackets, there wasn't a lot. They took it. There was an open truck, and they threw everything on there. We had certain pillows that we used, that a tailor uses, to press on, like you would use today on an ironing board. They ripped them open; they were looking for money hidden there. Of course there was none. They looked for other items of value and when they finished, they just stripped the store to the walls. Scissors, knives, anything they thought would be of interest that they could possibly resell, make a few dollars on, they took. And there was a worktable, and on that worktable there was a pin cushion that a tailor uses to put their needles and pins into it, and my mother was sitting near the table, white in the face. I stood next to her. [One of the men] had a smirk on his face. He picked up the pin cushion and handed it to my mother. He said, 'Superstition has it that if you remove a pin cushion from someone's house, you will destroy the friendship that goes with it.' So he handed it to my mother, clicked his heels and turned around and got into the truck and they drove off. So my mother sat there with tears. I looked at her. There's very little that anyone could say, so we took a few moments until she regained her composure and we closed the doors and went upstairs to our apartment."[35]

✡ Are They Going to Burn Us? ✡

Dorrit St. John lived in a condominium in Vienna. The building was partly owned by the consul general of Guatemala, and the consulate was on the property so the building had the country's insignia on the outside and the Guatemalan flag flying over the building. "Because we lived on a main thoroughfare, I was able to watch a lot of the things that happened from a window. You could see the trucks going by filled with people and I said, 'Mama, what is happening?' And she said to me, 'You children get dressed in double clothing right now.' And we put on heavy clothing. My mother had a feeling they were going to come and pick us up any minute. It didn't take long. About an hour later, there was a terrible banging on the door. There were two or three SS men standing there with guns drawn. They said, 'Where's the Jew? Where are all the Jews?' My mother said my father isn't here. And they came in to look. They couldn't find my father. In the meantime, two other men rounded up all the people that lived in our building and, before we knew it, they herded all the people into our apartment."

Most people in the building were Jewish, but the SS also forced the consul general's mother into Dorrit's apartment. They locked about two dozen people in the room while they ransacked the other apartments.

As they locked the doors, Dorrit had heard them say, "We'll get to you guys later." Dorrit remembered thinking, "Are they going to burn us? Are they going to annihilate us? What are they going to do? Everybody was hysterical. There was one lady who kept saying, 'They're coming with the torches! They're gonna torch us! They're gonna burn us!' They barricaded the house, you couldn't get out."

Eight hours later, the consul general was finally located, and he told the intruders they were on foreign soil and had to leave the building. The Jews were released and went back to their homes to find they had been ransacked. "My father's business was ransacked. The mob just walked in—they came in the front door—ripped all the clothing, stripped the stores bare and ran. And nobody said anything. There was a Jewish star on the front of the store to indicate that's a Jewish business. 'Jude! Take whatever you want.' That's exactly what they did. That was on the 10th of November, that everything just went worse and worse and worse. Two or three days later, they brought four Jewish families over to our home and said, 'From now on, they live in your home. They have no more homes here, if you don't want them they'll just have to go out on the street.' Well, of course we took them in."[36]

✡ Lucky Lady ✡

Anni Reisner was a 12-year-old whose family moved to Vienna, Austria, after her father was forced to resign from his job in Stuttgart, Germany. Her mother came from a religious family, but her father didn't believe in organized religion, and she remembered having a Christmas tree until she was seven. When they moved to Austria, however, her mother sent Anni to Hebrew school. The private school in Vienna rejected her because she was Jewish, so she attended a private Jewish high school.

On Kristallnacht three Gestapo agents came to their home and demanded that Anni's mother hand over all her money and jewelry. Her mother asked when she could get everything back, and they said, "Lady, you should be glad we didn't throw your children out the window."[37]

✡ This Apartment Is Mine ✡

Kurt Füchsl was only seven years old and does not remember the details of Kristallnacht, but his mother told him what had happened. "An interior decorator had taken a picture of our beautiful living room and displayed this picture of our apartment in his shop window. A Frau Januba saw the picture and heard that we were Jewish. She came around to the apartment and asked if it was for sale. She was told it wasn't, but a few days later, on the morning of Kristallnacht, she came back with some officers and said, 'This apartment is now mine.' We were told we had to leave by six that evening. When my mother protested to the officers that she had a sick child at home who was already asleep they told her, 'All right, but you have to get out by six in the morning.'"[38]

✡ No Jews Here ✡

Werner Cohen lived in Essen on Brahmsstrasse, a street named after the composer Johannes Brahms. "I noticed a large crowd around the house. I walked up closer to the house. People were staring at me, stopping their conversation, kind of rubbernecking. Then they parted and I moved closer and saw there was a lot of broken items that had been thrown out of the window and smashed glass. I walked inside the house and there was my mother looking haggard with my little sister. I said, 'What's going on?' My mother informed me that earlier the Gestapo had been in the house and taken my father into custody.

"Later, a group of SA men had come. I was told when the Gestapo came, they knocked loudly on the door and said loudly, 'Are there any Jews here?' There were Jewish families on two other floors. When they got to the top floor, there were two spinster ladies and they said, 'There are no Jews here. We're catholic ladies.'

"My sister was hiding under the bed scared of what was going on. The damage was done by the SA thugs and my mother having related this to me said, 'I want you to go to your room on the third floor and hide because we don't know if the Gestapo is coming back or not.'

"An hour later I heard the clumping on the stairs and two guys knock at my door and say, 'Are you Werner Cohen?' I say, 'Yes.' Between the two guys I was marched down the stairs. All I remember is my knees buckled. I never had weak knees my whole life. I remember one of the guys asking if my father owned the house. He mumbled something and I thought it was something like, 'Us Gestapo agents don't have our own houses.' He felt like Jews had it all or something.

"I was only 16. I had no way of knowing what to think of it. I just went along with these guys. I couldn't have done anything to get away. They took me away to prison. When you're a young kid like I was you operate on two levels. On one hand, anything you do is exciting. You've never been in prison before and now you can see what it is like. On other hand, you're right there. I remember this reaction of 'how interesting' and, at the same time, 'What is this all about?' and 'How is this going to end?' They kept us in this municipal jail for a couple of days. It was overcrowded and they sent me to a suburb to a different jail where I stayed for a couple of days."[39]

✡ Taken from the Farm ✡

Henry Cohen was living and working in Silesia on an agricultural farm of Polish Jews on November 9 when a convoy of SS and SR [*sic*] men arrived. "We were working. They called us in from the field and locked us in the stables with the cows and the horses. They kept us in there for 24 hours—no food, no water, no sanitary facilities—while they were destroying the castle. They broke into it, broke all the windows, stole all the property. Every boy and girl had a bin and they stole all the property out of it. All males who were 16 and older were arrested and sent to a concentration camp. Maybe 25–30 people. They hauled them away without saying anything. The whole camp was devastated. We tried to clean up and do the best we could to get things back to normal. At some point we were notified all the men were coming back. And they did, with their heads shaven."[40]

✡ A Lucky Tip ✡

Nine-year-old Frank Correl took a streetcar and a long walk to get to his school in Frankfurt am Main. The city was home to some 35,000 Jews. "I didn't know anything particular was amiss on that day. I noticed catty-corner to the school there was a store where the windows were all smashed, the merchandise was lying in the street, people were standing around. They said these were Jewish stores being smashed. We were called to an assembly as we had been for the Anschluss [Germany's annexation of Austria] and the Munich Agreement [signed by British Prime Minister Neville Chamberlain] on the Sudetenland. One teacher was in a brownshirt stormtrooper uniform. He told us how Jews were in the process of destroying Germany and Germany had to resist the overwhelming force of world Jewry. Then we were all sent home.

"My heart was in my throat. I walked to the street car and saw the blackened front of the synagogue. Obviously, a fire had been set. The synagogue was about two blocks from the school. I remember a butcher shop with smashed windows and glass lying all over the ground."

When Correl got home, he told his mother and aunt all that he had witnessed. "My mother tried to calm me down. It wasn't till much later that I found out what happened at the house that day. My father was out of Germany, he had gotten out literally the afternoon of Kristallnacht because he'd gotten a tip from the Gestapo. My mother had come back to town earlier in the evening. Apparently, after I left for school, the Gestapo stopped at the house as part of a roundup of Jews looking for my father and my uncle, who was a mining engineer. My uncle was out of town on the tip, but had gone to Berlin because he wasn't able to leave Germany and thought it was safer in the bigger city."[41]

✡ Seen and Not Heard ✡

Thirteen-year-old Lucille Eichengreen related her experience in Hamburg: "Germans burned all synagogues; they burned the books, the Torah. They set fire to Jewish stores, smashed the front of Jewish stores. There was a big Jewish department store and the merchandise was swimming in the canals. The following morning, the men were picked up and were taken to Oranienburg and Sachsenhausen, and were detained anywhere between six weeks and six months. All returned with shaven heads and had rumpled suits from disinfecting machines. Most who returned left Germany but would not tell us what had happened, what it was like. As a child I realized something was not right, but our upbringing at that time was that we were to be seen and not heard."[42]

✡ Chicken for Dinner ✡

Therese Gertrude Isenberg was about to turn 18. She lived in Ober-Ramstadt, a small town in Hesse, Germany, and was on her way to Darmstadt. "I went out the back door and I saw 4–5 people running, gasping for air. I didn't pay attention and went around the corner. The lady on the corner, Mrs. Kiplinger, saw me and said, 'Trude, your synagogue is burning.' And I said to her, 'Well, let it burn.' I guess this was my reaction."

Therese went to her uncle's house and saw her cousin Julius and asked him if she should go to Darmstadt. He could see the synagogue from his house, and saw something burning, but told her he thought it was safe to go on the train to Darmstadt.

Therese met her cousin Alice and went with her to Darmstadt. Alice went to a place where she learned how to be a dressmaker, and Therese decided to go to the home of another family. "I told them what happened and they said, 'Don't go anywhere. Just stay with us.'

"At 12 o'clock noon, they rounded up all the Jewish men. They came with garbage trucks and rounded up all the Jewish men. We heard the sirens. There were two beautiful synagogues in Darmstadt and word got around that they were burning the synagogues."

Around 5 p.m. Alice came for Therese, and they decided to return home. When she got to her house, Therese was surprised to find her father preparing dinner. She asked him what he was doing home, and he said the mayor had sent out a message that Jewish men should stay in their homes; otherwise, they would be sent to Buchenwald.

"I said, 'What are you doing?'

"He said, 'I killed a chicken. You have a birthday,' which was November 12, 'and we're going to have chicken for dinner.'"

At dusk, Therese's family was joined by her uncle and his wife, her cousin Julius, and his brother Manfred. "They couldn't stay in their house, everything was destroyed. We didn't know where my grandmother was. We just didn't know. . . . So here were seven people in the bedroom on a cold night. Our bedroom was adjoining the bedroom of the gentile people who rented our house and he was a Nazi. So we didn't dare make any noise because if word got out that my father hadn't been sent anyplace, god knows what he would have done. So we were lying there in bed, when we hear the Nazis, the stormtroopers running, running, hollering and screaming.

"My uncle had a butcher shop. In those days there was an ordinance that before you killed kosher, you had to have a gun to hit the animal and get the cow unconscious before you could slaughter it. So my cousin Manfred started hollering, 'We have a gun in the house. If they find the gun, they're going to come and kill us.' [It was illegal for Jews to possess weapons.] My mother was lying there half paralyzed. It was a night you never forget.

"Morning came and my aunt finally went down and found my grandmother. My grandmother went to a nephew and niece. She went to her room and they didn't touch it. They knew an old woman was in there, but the rest of the house was destroyed. The mayor sent word they could be seen again on the street. Apparently men who were taken hadn't been taken to a concentration camp, just to a jail and they'd been released. My friend's house had been burned down. We were spared. But after that we knew this was the end, the beginning of it."[43]

✡ Come and Help Us! ✡

Kurt Maier was just eight years old when a crowd gathered outside his house in the German town of Kippenheim and began to throw rocks through the window. "They smashed against the door downstairs and my mother and I hid under an overturned bathtub. We had a moveable bathtub and we turned it over so we wouldn't be hit by rocks. I think by that time they had rounded up all adults, including my grandfather, who had had a stroke and was shaking. My father wasn't there. I think it was late afternoon. I heard that the synagogue was on fire, but I didn't go on the street to see the fire. After awhile we heard a whistle blow and the crowd dispersed. This must have been orchestrated. I was very frightened.

"I remember at night sleeping upstairs. Everything was quiet and all of a sudden my mother said, 'Someone is downstairs, someone is downstairs.' . . . My mother called a neighbor, a German farmer who lived behind us, Emil Ehret. She called out, 'Emil, Emil, come and help us, someone is here.' And he came running and chased the fellow away. We never found out who it was but suspected it was another person from down the street who was home and decided to take advantage and see what he could loot from a Jewish house."[44]

✡ Saved from a Wardrobe ✡

Susan was a teenager living in Nuremberg when her life changed. "That night I woke up to noise, shouting and screaming. About eight young storm troopers, drunk or crazed in some other way, smashed up our home. By the time they came into the bedroom I shared with my younger sister, they had done a lot of damage to other rooms and had locked my parents into their bathroom. My parents were terrified for their children and I could hear them screaming and shouting and then I became very frightened. I could not imagine what was happening to them.

"When the storm troopers came into our room, they pulled me out of bed. . . . As a 15-year-old, I was above all embarrassed. They then told me to get dressed and to get my clothes out of my wardrobe. This was of the heavy, continental type. When I stood in front of it, the eight young men threw it over. No doubt this was to kill me and they left the room.

"Luckily, there was so much destruction in the room, that a table, previously turned upside down, held the wardrobe at an angle long enough for me to wriggle out from underneath.

"My concern was also for my little sister. She had crawled under her blankets, and her bed was completely covered with broken glass, but she was all right. . . . Our elderly maid could not believe that Hitler, whom she admired, could be responsible for anything like this."[45]

✡ Destruction from 10 to 12 ✡

Eleven-year-old Lothar Molton was living in Hamburg, Germany's second largest city. He has no doubt that the violence was

35

premeditated. "Kristallnacht was a complete, organized destruction. It was not a spontaneous eruption by the population. It was pre-planned, exactly what is going to be hit, what is going to be destroyed, what is going to be left. And especially so in a town like Hamburg, which is very civil and comparable to other towns in Germany, small liberal towns in Germany. To my knowledge, no individual homes or houses were attacked in the city of Hamburg. The places that were attacked and destroyed were the temples and synagogues, and they were destroyed very thoroughly. The main synagogue of Hamburg was almost completely destroyed on the inside. The benches were overthrown. The Torahs were thrown out and set afire. But our Talmud Torah school right next door to this temple was not touched at all. So when we heard about the destruction, we did not go to school the next day. But we did go back to school very soon thereafter, and life continued as it had before, except that all the houses of worship did not exist anymore. That's the way Germany worked. Everything was very orderly. Destruction from 10 to 12, or 10 to 7, normal life the next day."[46]

✡ Book Burning ✡

Hans Waizner was only nine years old but remembered being forced to move from his family's home in Vienna to his grandmother's house. He and his mother were riding in a truck, filled with their possessions, driving through the city where they saw Jewish stores that had been vandalized. Upon reaching his grandmother's street, they saw a crowd throwing books out of a Jewish school into the street and burning them. "My strongest, most physical memory of Kristallnacht was of our lorry bumping and rolling across that pile of smoldering religious books. I will never forget it."[47]

✡ God Listened to Our Prayers ✡

Eleven-year-old Alexander Lebenstein remembered strangers running into his house in the small town of Haltern. They told the family to get out of the way and began taking their furniture and other possessions into the street. "From upstairs I heard my parents' bedroom falling through the window into the street. Dinnerware, glassware was being thrown out from the upper window, lower window. People were outside taking some things. Others were destroying or breaking up the furniture. We were all very, very frightened, needless to say, completely helpless."

Lebenstein remembers going with his family to the cemetery to hide because they were sure the Nazis would not come to the cemetery. Later that evening, they heard noises. "A whole group of people came storming into the cemetery. And we thought that they really were coming for us, that we were sold out, and we huddled together very frightened. There were two other people, two or three other people, I don't remember exactly, from the community with us hiding here. And we just huddled together and prayed. I guess that time God really listened to our prayers because these Nazis came to destroy and desecrate the cemetery, to destroy the stones. And that's exactly what they did. They plundered the stones; they broke up the stones, the memorials. They stampeded over the graves, and suddenly they left, and they were satisfied how they destroyed the cemetery and they left, and they didn't find us. So we were saved for that night."[48]

✡ We Don't Sell to Jews ✡

Inge Angst was a ninth-grade student in Mannheim at the time of Kristallnacht. She remembers that on November 10 her father was picked up. Later, the family learned the men had gone through Dachau and were taken to Sachsenhausen. This was only the beginning of Inge's nightmare.

"Around 10 o'clock they came and smashed the store. They were not in uniform. They wanted it to look like the people were mad because this guy in Paris was murdered. They had axes and all sorts of tools that they smashed the shelves and the merchandise [with]. They left after it was all done." Inge said the salesgirls from the store did not run away, they helped clean up and later acted as witnesses for the family after the war.

The ordeal was not over. "A couple of hours later, they came in uniform and went upstairs into our apartment. And they had trucks. They took away the merchandise into a restaurant nearby because they thought it belonged to them now. They took everything they could find that had any value, like silver Kiddush cups and any money they could find. They took our piggy banks. We were left without any money. They took the safe from the store and put it in the courtyard and had someone break into it because they thought there was a lot of money in it, but there wasn't. But our books were in there and they took the books. They didn't know my mother had the books in her head.

"We didn't have any money to buy food or anything. My mother made a list of what she thought people owed us and Mark and I went out and collected a few dollars. But we couldn't buy anything any way in the first few days because the SR [*sic*] were standing guard around the clock. . . . I asked the guard if I could go out and get some food and the guard said okay. But when I got to the store there were big red signs that said, 'We don't sell to Jews.'"[49]

✡ Children's Pajamas ✡

Lore Rosen also lived in Mannheim and was going off to school. "When I got downstairs, there was a small grocery store around the corner, and the lady who owned the store, she came running up to me and she said, 'Go upstairs and get your mother and go hide in the hospital or the old home for the aging because they're breaking up every store, they're taking away all the men, they're beating up people like crazy and you just go and get your mother and get out of there.' And I went upstairs and told my mother and I remember we ran like crazy to the Jewish hospital, and my mother volunteered her help and I don't know, I guess I just sat around scared. A lot of men, they hid them underneath sacks of potatoes, and they were safe. They didn't have to go to concentration camps while the others were picked up. We spent a terrible day hiding. They never came near the Jewish hospital, nor the Jewish home for the aging. They didn't touch that.

"When we got back, our neighbor, a very nice lady who has known my mother for hundreds of years, said, 'They came to your apartment looking for men.' And she had a key and said, 'I'll let you in. There's only a woman and her daughter who is a little girl.' And they opened all the drawers and threw everything on the floor. Some of my pajamas looked like boys' pajamas and they said to our neighbor, 'There must be a man here, there are pajamas.' And she said, 'No way, those are children's pajamas. A little girl wears them.' And they didn't take anything, they just threw everything upside down. And they didn't break anything."[50]

✡ Unhappy Birthdays ✡

Peter Ney remembered he was looking forward to November 11 because it was going to be his seventh birthday. He woke up to what sounded like barrels falling down the staircase in the apartment house. "I remember waking up, and on the side of my bed was a little bench, and in the year before, the way my parents had celebrated my birthday is they had this bench, and would put some presents on the bench during the night. I was somewhat confused, with the sound of the barrels going down, and all the excitement, and of my birthday, and I looked at the bench, and there wasn't anything on the bench. The room was still dark, and then the lights came on in my room, but I was already awake. And I was totally confused what was going on.

"When the lights went on, my mother had come into the room. She grabbed me. I think she grabbed the clothes. I don't think she got the clothes on me. I remember there was a room in the apartment, which was sort of a library, and there were big bookcases with very dark wood, and the bookcases, I think, ran from the floor to the ceiling, and the bookcases had been pulled from the wall and were lying across the room. They hadn't fallen on their face because there was other furniture there that was holding it up. There were books all over the place. My father also had liquor in that bookcase, there was like a liquor cabinet in there, and there were broken bottles of liquor all over the place. That's the first thing that I saw.

"I saw my father talking to some men in uniform. I remember he was standing there holding his Iron Cross that he had gotten in the First World War, and then we were chased out of the apartment and we had to go up to the attic. The apartment house I think had four floors and it had a peaked roof, and there was an attic there, and all the people from the apartment house were at the front of the attic. The attic as I remember had sort of a gate in front of it, and we were on the top area just before that gate on the stairs.

"When we were up in that attic area, it seemed like for a long time, and there was of course a lot of noise down below, and people screaming, and things were thrown out windows, furniture was smashed. And then things got quieter, and then I remember people came downstairs into their apartment to survey the damage. I don't think that anything in my room that I can recall was out of order. I mean it seemed as if they had skipped that room."

Peter's parents brought him into their bedroom. They had two mattresses that came together with a little space between them. This was the special place where they would sometimes let him sleep as a treat. They called it the *grabbala*. On Kristallnacht his parents said he could sleep in the grabbala. The problem was that a light fixture at the head of the bed had been shattered and glass was all over the bed, so they first had to clean the glass from the bed. "To me it was sort of unreal," Peter said. "I had woken out of a dream. I had thought about my birthday. I had heard these crashing sounds, and the sound of barrels going down the staircase. I mean, I really didn't even know whether this was real. The next day the police came, if you can believe it. The police came, and they took statements, and they filled out papers, and they did forms, as if they were going to do something about it. I found out later that they, the German government, had passed an emergency regulation which made sure that the insurance companies wouldn't have to pay for any of the damage. They were very efficient. They never left a stone unturned."[51]

Kristallnacht was also memorable for Fred Katz, who was turning 11 years old. "I was born on November 10th. The events took place on the 9th to the 10th so I couldn't very well ignore it. During the daytime on the 9th, suddenly a lot of cars came from outside. Nobody owned cars in my village [Oberlauringen]. So cars came up, and people came out who arrested all the Jewish men, including my brother. My brother was then 17. All the Jewish men were suddenly taken away. I mean, we had heard about the events that led up to Kristallnacht in terms that a German embassy official in France had been assassinated by a Jew, so we knew there were things in the air. But we didn't know what was happening. So, during the daytime, all of a sudden, all the Jewish men were arrested, and we were terribly scared. And my mother and I—my sister had already left for America and my brother was taken away—went to the neighbor's house. We hid in their attic in the evening. And then, during the night, we heard cars come up and people started smashing buildings and smashing the front door of the place in the house where I lived. And then we also heard them—since our house was right next door—we heard them smashing our house. Lots of noise and broken glass, and people yelling, 'Where are the Jews?' We were in terror, wondering, 'Are they going to find us and kill us?' So we stayed until the next morning.

"They got quiet after what seemed like a few hours and, in the morning, we crawled out and over rubble. All the windows were smashed. All the doors were smashed. The front doors were smashed. The furniture was smashed. We had this German furniture with a high glass front. These were all smashed, the glass smashed, toppled over. And thick German bedding was all ripped open, and stuff all over, feathers, feather bedding and all that.

"One of the striking things at that point for me was that none of the Christian families came. Nobody came. We were totally alone."[52]

November 10 was Rita Braumann's 12th birthday. That day in Cologne her girlfriend Helga came to wish her a happy birthday. "She was still at our place when the doorbell rang at 10:30 a.m. My father, who had meanwhile pinned his wartime decorations to his lapel, opened the front door. There stood several storm troopers, who asked politely: 'Are you Braumann? Is this house your property and is this your family?' When he told them Helga was my friend, they turned to this blonde and blue-eyed girl and said, 'You couldn't be Jewish too?' When she nodded, they yelled, 'Get yourself home.' She burst into tears and ran. To us they said politely, 'Go upstairs to your bedrooms' . . . then we heard the systematic destruction of all our furniture with tools they must have brought up from the cellar, because they were not carrying anything when they arrived. The noise was terrifying. We

43

went on the balcony, neighbors were on theirs and wanted to know what was happening, but we were too frightened to reply. Finally there was silence. The sight that awaited us downstairs was unbelievable. Absolutely everything had been demolished. . . . Suddenly, the telephone rang. . . . it was the mother of one of my school friends to inquire whether my scheduled birthday party was still taking place that afternoon! In all this debris stood my new three-speed bike, only slightly damaged but never to be used by me."[53]

✡ Something Bad Is Coming Down ✡

Jill Pauly said that no one anticipated what was to come on Kristallnacht. "There may have been indications in other parts of the country, but I don't think the press was as open and, if it was, the Jews just didn't believe it. And certainly they knew nothing because you don't send a 9-year-old on a train to Yeshiva in Cologne on the day that there's going to be such a deadly pogrom. So they just didn't know anything."

Jill's mother told her later that while she was at school a man from the police came to their house and warned the men not to go to the synagogue because "something bad is coming down." He didn't tell them any more, but it was enough to convince them not to go. A little while later, Jill's sister came home. "My mother said, 'What are you doing home?' She said, 'I got to school and there were a lot of Gestapo in front of the school, and they told me, "Little girl, go home. There'll be no school today." So I just went back to the train and came home.'

"At that point, my parents' phone started ringing and ringing and ringing. And my father and my uncle started screaming. They were fighting probably about how to do things. And they were hysterical, and very emotional, and my grandfather was very emotional. They were really, really out of it, with fear. The families called and told them to leave town. The destruction had started. They were calling from all over. From Gemunchenglattblatt, from Cologne, from Krearfeld, and from in town. And then my father got on the phone and started calling the Jewish people in town to tell them what he heard. He told them to get out. They were running away and we should do the same thing.

"They were afraid that they were collecting people in the shul and they would be picked up. My father had an inkling. And my grandfather. Then they heard from Demultzheim and they heard that grandmother got out of her sick bed, took the pictures of her grand-daughters off the wall and told her daughters, 'We are leaving!' And then they started ordering the cars. I remember that, and I remember distinctly that my uncle George wanted to go out to close the shutters. And my grandmother screamed at him, 'Stop closing the shutters, it's too late for that!' And then when we got the message that we were leaving and running away. I wanted to take my favorite things. I had gotten a new pair of shoes, and my favorite doll. And my sister wanted to take her Shaddai, her silver Shaddai. And guess what? I had hidden it. And she couldn't find it. She screamed. She wasn't leaving without her Shaddai. And I went right to the hiding place and found it for her, I remember that. [Laughs] I don't know why I hid it, she probably hid something of mine.

"My father called his non-Jewish friends and said, 'Get my family out.' We were exiting, my mother and my father and my uncle

George were exiting the front door of the house, and the Nazi destroy-
ers were coming in the back door. So they didn't leave a minute too
soon. Because had they caught them, they would have taken them to
shul, and what they were doing with them in shul is they picked up
all the men, and they took them to Dachau and to Buchenwald.

"We were put in a car at about three o'clock. Three, four o'clock.
It was getting dusky. We screamed when we were separated from our
mother, especially me. And my grandmother was in the car with my
grandfather. My grandmother was in a cast. She had broken her leg.
They took us in the car and they couldn't calm us down because the
shul was two blocks away and we saw the fire. It terrified us. So we
had panic attacks. We were terrified. So my grandmother put us on
the ground of the car and put her feet on us. And we didn't see anything. It's not true, I did sneak up and I saw more burning on the way.
They took us to Cologne. I remember the relief getting out of that car
going to my aunt's and uncle's house. But I was very frightened. I was
terribly frightened.

"The men in the family decided not to go anywhere for 24 hours
after Kristallnacht. They stayed in a car and drove. And drove and
drove and drove and only took gas where they knew the gas attendants weren't Nazis. So that's how they survived the first 24 hours.
And then things calmed down again. Because the German people
really objected to Mr. Hitler about Crystal Night. It disturbed their
sense of order. To have all those broken glass and screaming people
and plunder. They didn't like that. He could do what he wanted to do
with the Jews, but do it systematically please, and do it clandestinely
or whatever you want to do, but don't disturb our way of life. So things
quieted down that way.

"My father was petrified. I still think that that's what saved us. Their fear. Not everybody was as frightened as they were. And we got away."[54]

✡ Bowling for Jews ✡

Ingrid Komar was 11 years old and remembers the Gestapo coming to her house in Frankfurt am Main. "There were two plainclothes men, just like out of the movies, the trench coat and the whole bit. They followed my father into the bathroom. I think they were afraid that he was going to swallow some pills or cut his throat, I don't know what, but the next thing I knew, he was leaving with them.

This was the night the synagogues burned. I remember my mother and I going to my uncle Willie's house. He was taken away too. And his wife was in hysterics.

"I also remember that I went to school that day. To the Jewish school. I think in the Jewish school we were told what was going on, like the synagogues were burning and people were smashing Jewish establishments and attacking houses, and so they decided they would send us home. We were all called into an assembly, and we were told we were going to be let go two by two, because they didn't want to call attention to all these children, schoolchildren, leaving school at the same time. It was not a time when children were supposed to be on the streets. It was early in the day. And I remember having to go home on the street car. Usually, I was picked up by the chauffeur. I was terrified because maybe there were twenty Jewish kids on this street car and I was not supposed to be on the street. But we got home, and then my mother decided we would go to the factory, the sausage factory, because the sausage factory was closed, and she figured that we would be safe. Wrong guess.

"We no sooner got there then this mob came down the street and started smashing the doors and the windows. The factory was tiled. It was very clean, like a bathroom. The whole floor and ceiling, everything was tiled. My father had stored his bowling equipment there, and they took a bowling ball, and smashed all the tiles. My mother and I fled upstairs. The mob was smashing the tile, and also marble, with the bowling ball. It sounded like the world was coming to an end. It sounded like an earthquake. And it was really terrifying.

"And the other thing that happened was that . . . when I was born, my father bought a wine. I'm not sure if the vintage was the year that I was born or some earlier vintage. Anyway, there was a case of that wine around and these idiots took that wine, the whole case of it, and smashed it in the courtyard. And that's when my mother became hysterical, because when she smelled all that alcohol, she thought they were setting the building on fire. We were upstairs. There was some kind of awning. If you operated it from inside the room, it came down in one piece. Well, my mother was standing on the windowsill and she wanted to jump. And I pulled the awning. She'd lost it at that point. . . . But she snapped to very quickly."[55]

✡ Chunks of Beard ✡

"You didn't have TV or radio or things like that in those days that you could know what was happening with quick news flashes," recalled

Harry Spector of his childhood in Leipzig, the largest city in Saxony. "So it wasn't until the next morning that everybody began to realize what had happened. On my way to school that morning, I had about a 15–20 minute walk to school, I didn't see much of anything. They sent us back home. I went back another way and I saw they had gathered some of the Jews. One man in particular had a beard, and I saw one of these stormtroopers pull his beard and pull chunks of beard in his hand. That stayed with me all these years."[56]

Harry Alexander was also living in Leipzig and had a similar experience. At about four o'clock in the morning there was a knock on the door. "A Jewish boy, about 16–17 years old, a friend of my big brother Bernie knocked on the door and said, 'Help us, they're killing Jews.' Sure enough they came to our house, broke down the door. Perverts, bums, German bums, convicts that they let out of the jail with their knives that said 'Blood and Honor' on it. They beat everybody up. They arrested my brother Paul. Bernie had gotten wind of it and he had left the day before. He went to Paris. He had taken a train. That was when the Gestapo came and said, 'Where is Bernie?' My mother said she didn't know, that he doesn't always come home. They broke all the furniture, they broke all the dishes. They took the feather beds and shook them out the window and made believe it was Christmas, that it was snowing. They destroyed everything in their path. They took Jewish girls and raped them in the streets. They dragged Jews by their beards through the streets. They started burning synagogues, burning books, putting fire to Jewish stores. All hell broke loose and no one knew what was going on. I was beat up too. We didn't know where to hide. My little sister hid under the bed. After the destruction, they finally left. We still heard the screams. There was blood flowing in the streets. My mother told me to get a loaf of bread and come right back. I went out and a car came screeching to a halt and they said, 'Jewish dog, get in,' and I was arrested and taken to jail. I was in cell #10. I'll never forget it. Paul was sent to Buchenwald. My mother somehow got Paul out of Buchenwald. To this day, I don't know how she did it."[57]

✡ In the School It Was Horror ✡

Carola Steinhardt was in a boarding school. "The Germans came and threw all the kids out, cut into the feather beds, and the whole school was in an uproar. The little kids were crying, looking for their parents. But naturally there were no parents; it was a boarding school. And, well, I was one of the older ones, there were six-year-olds; we held onto them. And they marched us to the mayor's office with the teachers, and the teachers were frightened themselves. We thought we were going to be shot there, but we weren't. We stayed there for a while, and from there we went back home. In the school it was horror. All the feather beds and everything was on the floor and all the—it was a religious school—so the Torah cloths were all torn and the books all, whatever. But we remained in the school until 1939. We fixed it up again, and we stayed there."[58]

✡ Little Did I Know ✡

Edith Trzeciak was a child in Stuttgart. "My stepfather told me to get dressed and we took the streetcar to as close as we could to downtown. I remember a lot of fire and smoke and it scared me. All the big stores had broken windows and fire and smoke. I had never been near a fire before. There was a lot of noise, shouting and screaming, and some 'bad' words I had never heard before. There were men in uniform and Dad told me not to be scared. He was crying, and I vaguely remember seeing some other people cry too. But a whole lot were cheering and yelling, 'Heil Hitler.' . . . I had one fear, that some kids I knew would see me and laugh at me, because my Dad was carrying me like a baby and hugging me close to him. And I do recall seeing some kids whom I knew in Hitler Youth and BDM [League of German Girls] uniforms. Not being one of them was the great tragedy of my life at that age, and now they would see me like a baby. Little did I know how lucky I was."[59]

✡ Treated Like a Dog ✡

Lotte Kramer attended a school in the Liberal Synagogue in Mainz. Before leaving for school, her cousin called and told her to stay home because the synagogue was on fire. She also warned Lotte to tell her father to hide because all the men were being taken to concentration camps. Lotte's father hid in the woods until nightfall and then returned home and began calling other members of the family to check on them. Lotte's father found that his brother had been beaten and led through the street on a leash like a dog.[60] Altogether six synagogues were destroyed in Mainz.

✡ They Ruined Our Store ✡

Marga Hauptman was a 13-year-old living in Mannheim. "We heard rumors that in other towns something had happened. The morning of November 10 we realized something was going to happen. About 7–7:15 in the morning we heard footsteps stomping on the staircase leading to the second floor of our house. They banged at the door and yelled, 'Mr. Forcheimer, get dressed, you're coming with us.' Papa dressed as fast as he could and mama tried to give him a roll or something. They arrested him along with the other Jewish teenagers and men they could get a hold of. Most were taken to concentration camps, mostly Buchenwald and Dachau. My father ended up in Dachau.

"Shortly thereafter we realized there was another couple, an older couple, in their 60s living near us. My mother, always being concerned with others, said my sister and I should go over to this other couple and try to comfort this woman. No sooner did we get there when the telephone rang and mama said, 'Get home quick. Get home quick. We have problems. They ruined our store.' So we dashed back.

"As we got back into the street where our store was we saw my mother had already gotten the people from the store to sweep up all the broken windows and everything they had kicked out into the street. Since there is a German law that you can't leave the street with litter, she was afraid of all that. She got them to clean up immediately and sweep up all of the glass.

"A little while later we were sitting upstairs in our anteroom, which had a full glass wall bordering onto the staircase, and we again heard the heavy footsteps and bang, bang, bang at the door. They started swarming into the apartment. They looked for money and dashed around like wild looking for money. They stole the piggy banks and we were left with no money whatsoever. They dashed to the living room and a bookcase that had glass doors. They opened up the bookcases and took every last book and threw them out the windows. Someone else was downstairs and put a match to it so everything that was in that bookcase burned to a crisp. There were pictures, mementos, very fine books; there was Schiller and Goethe, which was, after all, their big thing. They all burned to a crisp, with two exceptions. One was the book that was by Heinrich Heine, who was, of course, a Jewish writer. That was the only book that we brought out that was untouched. The other was a book that listed all of the Jewish German soldiers that had been killed during World War I. Those were the only two books that we pulled out of the ashes. Once they were burned, they immediately told us we had to clean the streets because there was a streetcar coming by. Have you ever tried to put ashes in something when you're not prepared for it? It was unbelievable.

"After that, they did not leave. They had, of course, smashed the entire business. We had yard goods and things like that. Since everything was smashed they decided they had to confiscate the merchandise. So it took them I don't know how long to carry the merchandise in a truck to a nearby hall that was being used as a dance hall. They carried every ounce of merchandise and carried it into that dance hall. But that wasn't enough. They wanted more. So they questioned my mother that she should give them the combination of the safe, which was, of course, locked. My mother said, 'I'm terribly sorry but I don't know the combination of the safe. You took my husband away; he is the only one who knows the combination of the safe.' Well, smart they obviously were not. They took the safe out of the store and somehow managed to get it into the courtyard, which was part of our house and started working on it with torches, and they worked on it for a solid three or four hours before they managed to get the safe open. Of course, their main reasoning was that they wanted money, but there was not too much in it. Secondly, they wanted all the information about people who might have still dealt with this Jewish store, so they wanted the names of people who might have been our customers. It took them until dark to finish and then the safe was totally and completely damaged. We didn't have a nickel to our names.

"They decided to guard us for the next 10 days. I think we were the only Jewish family in the entire town that was guarded by the SR [*sic*] or the SS. So we used to get fresh rolls hung on the door in the morning. Needless to say, no one was willing to bring us rolls or milk or anything so we had to rely on a maid who snuck everything in at night. She paid for it because we didn't have any money."[61]

CHAPTER 3

Coming of Age, and Heroes of Another Age

O ne of the most important life cycle events for a young Jewish boy and his family is the celebration of his bar mitzvah. A Jewish boy automatically becomes a bar mitzvah upon reaching the age of 13. According to tradition, a Jew becomes a man at this age and is expected to fulfill the requirements of Jewish law. Though not mandatory, a bar mitzvah ceremony is typically conducted to formally recognize the boy's assumption of his obligations. He is also given the right to take part in leading religious services, to count in a minyán (the minimum number of people needed to perform certain parts of religious services), to form binding contracts, to testify before religious courts, and to marry. Ordinarily the bar mitzvah is one of the happiest days of a boy's life, but for these Jews it was a nightmare they will never forget.

Girls at the age of 12 (sometimes 13) whose families are in the Reform, Conservative, or Reconstructionist movement now typically celebrate a *bat* mitzvah. In the 1930s, however, this was a very rare occurrence, and to this day Orthodox Jews do not have bat mitzvahs. As a result, the Germans and Austrians in this chapter who were reaching this milestone in their life during and around the time of Kristallnacht were boys.

Though the 13th birthday had particular significance because of the religious celebration, many boys and girls had other birthdays that became unforgettable because they occurred at the time of the pogroms.

✡ Remember ✡

Sigi Hart was preparing for his bar mitzvah in Berlin. On November 9 he headed for school and saw smoke and fires. "They started to break the windows of the Jewish stores, they took out the merchandise. They brought big, big picket signs, 'Don't buy from the Jews.' They started burning the synagogues."

Hart returned home without going to school. His parents decided to send his brother out to see what was happening because he looked Aryan rather than Jewish, with blonde hair and blue eyes. "He came back and said in the stores that belong to the Jews, windows were broken and people were walking in and out as if it were their own. And the temples were burned. Everyone was invited to temple and we didn't know what to do."

The person who took care of the synagogue had a little house in the back that was not destroyed in the fire. The week after Kristallnacht he offered to let the Harts use it for the bar mitzvah. "We came Saturday morning to this place. We had about three or four people standing outside watching if they saw any police or SS or Nazis coming [so] we could escape from the backyard. In one corner were the burned Torah scrolls, they were lying on the floor covered [Hart breaks down as he recalls the scene]. I said my *bracha* [prayer]. I did what I had to do for my bar mitzvah. This was supposed to be my happiest day. The rabbi was standing there crying. He told me when he made a *bracha*, 'Remember, never forget.' This was my bar mitzvah, 1938. We went home and my parents decided this is not a life to continue."[62]

✡ They Stole My Bike ✡

Ernest Marx never had a chance to celebrate his bar mitzvah in his home town of Speyer. "My bar mitzvah was supposed to be on November 19th, 1938. I was in Dachau. I never heard the name Kristallnacht until I came to this country. To us it was the 9th of November. It was still one of the worst nights of my life. I saw the flames of our synagogue, which I'll never forget. It was only a few blocks from us." Marx said he "experienced fear of living" as he watched people break into the kosher butcher and ransack stores. "I saw the flames, I heard the sirens. I saw the firemen going by, but they didn't put out the fire. They were protecting the other houses of the Christians. The Hitler Youth had on uniforms, with an arm band with a swastika. I was told to get away from the window."

Marx fondly recalled that his parents had hung up a new bicycle in the window. "It was amazing a kid of 13 would get a bicycle for his bar mitzvah. It was a shiny bicycle. Nobody ever got a bicycle for his bar mitzvah, a used one maybe, but this was like getting a Cadillac.

"That night two men from the Gestapo came and arrested my father. I think he knew them, being in a small town. He asked them, 'Why am I being arrested?' They said, 'None of your damn business.

Pack a suitcase for an overnight stay.' My mother was hysterical. He was told to take one of his two sons and he picked me. To this day I don't know why my father took me. I have come to the conclusion either he loved me more than my brother or he wanted my brother to stay with my mother as a protector. We were taken to the police headquarters down the street. Sixty to eighty Jewish people were assembled. We were shoved into a bus. They gave us something to eat, I think a sort of a sandwich. My father was orthodox and wouldn't eat it because it wasn't kosher. He told me to eat it. I think it was just a slice of bread with butter or something. We rode all night in the bus and came to the most feared camp in Germany at that time—Dachau.

"There was an expression, if you're not nice, you go to Dachau. If you had an argument with a Nazi, you were taken to Dachau. Everybody knew that. What do I know? I was 13. I was a dumb kid who loved to play soccer. I didn't think it was going to be the end of the world. When I came back from Dachau, the bike was gone. That was when I got mad at the Germans. They stole my bike."[63]

✡ Back to Poland ✡

Hugo Beckerman was in Berlin on November 9. "They started burning all the synagogues. All the stores were demolished. They went into apartments and threw things out the window, bedding. I was living with my parents. We lived in the back of my father's store. Nothing happened to us because my father had no sign indicating there was a shoe repair place upstairs. I saw how they broke the windows and plundered everything and threw it out on the street. Where we lived were all Jewish stores. I walked along the street during the action and watched. I had just become bar mitzvah. I looked in astonishment and thought, 'What is going on?' I realized later in the same year when they came to our house and got my father that everyone from Poland was picked up and sent back to Poland where they originally came from."[64]

✡ A Torah's Journey ✡

Frederick Firnbacher lived in Straubing. He was only eight and remembers that November 9 started as a normal day. Then the world turned upside down. "They went to our synagogue and ransacked it but couldn't burn it because it was in a residential neighborhood. Then they went around to the different houses where Jews lived and tried to break in. Our house had a very strong door and they weren't able to break in. Some of the neighbors stuck their heads out and told them to be quiet and to leave and finally they left.

"In the morning, the German police came to the house with an arrest warrant for my father and took him off to the local jail where he stayed for a couple of days. While he was there, he met all the other Jewish males and a couple of days later he was sent to Dachau. Meanwhile, at the synagogue (which was built in 1907), they had taken fire axes and torn up the synagogue and desecrated the Torahs and the prayer books, and the ark was a shambles. The Germans came back later and collected the different things and took them to police headquarters."

One of the items the Germans took was a Torah that belonged to Firnbacher's family. "My great grandfather had moved to the United States, struck gold, and returned to Germany a wealthy man. He hired a *sofer* [a scribe] to move into his house and write the weekly portion each week. It took an entire year and [the Torah] was ready in time for my grandfather's bar mitzvah in 1872. It was also used for my father's bar mitzvah. My dad later on went to the Gestapo because he had permission to take the Torah out of Germany to the United States. And luckily they gave it to him and said, 'Here, take it.' So they gave him some sort of permission. He carried the Torah through the snow. Just imagine a Jew in 1938 carrying a Torah through the streets of Germany. He brought it to the U.S. and I was bar mitzvahed out of it, and my son Michael was bar mitzvahed on the 100th anniversary of when it was written."[65] The Firnbacher scroll is now in Ohr Kodesh Congregation synagogue in Chevy Chase, Maryland.

✡ The Smell of Burning Parchment ✡

Arnold Fleischmann lived in Bayreuth but was staying with a family named Bloom in Nuremberg while he studied for his bar mitzvah. He recalled feeling confident in public places. "I wasn't afraid to get on a street car or going to school or walking the streets, even though we sometimes got into fights on the way to school. We kept our tennis shoes in our gym bags and would use our shoes to beat them back." Everything changed on Kristallnacht.

"We woke up to the sound of crashing. These huge Brownshirts with exposed daggers walked into our bedroom. We pretended to be asleep even though they turned the lights on. They didn't bother us. They walked back out. They smashed all the kitchen dishes and china closets, turned over the furniture and made sure just about everything was broken. Then they discovered that Mr. Bloom had a collection of *Sefer* Torahs [Torah scrolls] and a group of scrolls like the Megillah and they rolled the carpet back and started to burn them on the living room floor. To this day I will never forget the smell of burning parchment. Then they grabbed Tisha Bloom and took him away and left us crying in the middle of this total disaster.

"When I realized there was nothing I could do for the Blooms, I realized that something similar could have been happening at my house. They had ripped out the telephone. So I got dressed and took what money I had and went to a public telephone. This all happened at 3–4 a.m. By this time it was about 5 and I called my house in Bayreuth." His family's German housekeeper answered the phone and told Arnold his grandfather, father, and uncle had been picked up by storm troopers at three in the morning.

"They took them to the slaughterhouse and they were convinced they were going to be hung on meat hooks, something that did happen as you may know in Bucharest. They killed Jews and hung them on meat hooks. They didn't do that. They just kept them cold and fearful.

"They took my father to the city prison because he was a leader of the Jewish community at that point. As the leader of the Jewish community, they wanted him locked up.

"I took the first train I could find and went to Bayreuth and went to the house and by that time it was about 9 in the morning. We got clothes together and Margaret [the family maid] and I went to the slaughterhouse and picked up my uncle and grandfather and brought them home with us. They were permitted to leave. They were completely shaken up, morally and emotionally completely destroyed. Then I found out my father was at the city jail. Margaret gave me a thermos with some soup and some other food. Here I was a kid who just turned 13 on November 7. I took it to the city jail. The city jail administrator happened to be a classmate of my father in school and he was very decent to me and let me get into the jail cell.

"My father and Mr. Kahn, who was the vice president of the Jewish community, were locked up together. They were shaken up. They never believed something like that could happen in a Germany that was civilized, that believed in Goethe and Schiller. It was beyond their comprehension that something like that could happen. We could trace our family back in Germany longer than most Germans could. We had at least a 500-year history in Germany. My paternal ancestors came from Spain in 1492 but my mother's family might have been there even longer. We knew we had a history and a tie that was completely ruptured. After about a week my father was released."

Arnold's 13th birthday had been on November 7. His bar mitzvah was supposed to be November 12 in Nuremberg, but it didn't take place. The synagogues and schools were burned and very little of the Jewish community remained. "There was this total collapse of what it was like to be a Jew in Germany. . . . After Kristallnacht I was afraid. I had seen enough of the cruelty of the Nazis and the so-called innocent bystanders who had seen these things and done nothing."[66]

✡ "Celebrating" without Dad ✡

Henry Glaser had his bar mitzvah in Berlin on December 12, 1938. "My father was in a concentration camp. He was picked up on Kristallnacht. I went to school in the morning on Kristallnacht. We were told at 9 or 10 o'clock to go home. Synagogues were burning. Jewish store windows were smashed. I was coming home by bus from school. Everyone was in the apartment. I was relating what I saw. By 2 in the afternoon, the doorbell rang and three Gestapo men came and arrested my father. My brother asked if he could go in his place and they said, 'No, we want Max Glaser.' My mother was very upset. She called the person who had taken over my father's business after the Aryanization. He went to the police building and came back and said my father was arrested. By that time thousands of other German businessmen had been arrested. Within two or three days we knew he was in Sachsenhausen."[67]

✡ Germany's Heroes ✡

Jews were proud citizens of Germany, and thousands had fought and died for their country in World War I. Many had been honored for their heroism. In fact, of the 550,000 Jews in Germany in 1914, 100,000 fought in the Great War. About 12,000 German Jews lost their lives in the war, and about 35,000 were decorated for their service.[68] These patriots may have had the most difficult time comprehending the horror of Kristallnacht and what had become of the country they had fought so hard to protect.

✡ I Gave My Son to the Fatherland ✡

Arnold Fleischmann was studying for his bar mitzvah in Nuremberg and returned to his home in Bayreuth to discover much of his family was arrested. "Uncle Benno had managed to put his socks and pants on, and so did my father, but they took my grandfather in his bare feet and his night shirt and walked him through the streets. My grandfather told them, 'I gave my son to the fatherland.' My uncle Arthur had been killed in the First World War after he had been awarded the Iron Cross First Class and volunteered to go back. He was a first lieutenant who died on the western front. It killed my grandmother because she died out of grief. He said, 'I gave my son to the fatherland and this is how you treat me.' He couldn't understand. It was completely beyond his comprehension at that point."[69]

✡ I Am a German Soldier ✡

Alexander Lebenstein had just turned 11 years old a few days earlier when the news reached the small town of Haltern that in neighboring towns the Nazis had burned some synagogues, plundered private homes, broken up furniture, and beat and arrested people. "My father, being so strong, German-like, said it will never happen to him. It will never happen in his little town. After all, he had all his buddies around; he fought in the First World War, side by side with these men. He fought on the French border. He was highly decorated. Perhaps it could happen in the big towns, but not in this little town, not to him.

"So when my parents were informed that this was going on November 9th in some of the bigger cities, that synagogues were burning and homes were being plundered, I don't know if my father put on a façade, but I could sense he was frightened, my mother was frightened, of things that were going on. There was so much disturbing news coming out every day, every hour, and people would let us know, one could hear it on the radio. The propaganda was very strong, anti-Semitism was so strong, one could feel it in the air.

"So November 9th came and went. And like my father said, nothing would ever happen over here, and he was certainly right, on that day nothing happened. The next day, November 10th, some friends came and told him that a group of Nazis from neighboring towns came and they were organizing local Nazis, young people, and presently they were destroying the synagogue. They feared that they would come and do to the Jewish homes what they did in the big cities, that there was talk of it. By this time, it was too late for my father to do anything but to stay still. Where would he run?

"I guess he thought his buddies would come out with guns and fight off the Nazis. I don't know. So naïve, I guess. And suddenly the Nazis came down the street. I don't remember—thirty, forty, fifty— they came in bunches. And from far away they started throwing stones and breaking the glass, and the store window, and the other window in front of my house, upstairs through the bedroom.

"My father went into the house, and I don't even know how to tell this story. In a way, I feel very bad about it, but I can understand his pride. He went and put on his decorations from World War I on his chest, and he approached the Nazis in the street and he said, 'You cannot do this to me or my family. I am a German soldier, I earned these decorations.' They certainly didn't listen. They tore off these decorations from his chest and threw them into the street. They pushed him around. I, of course, was very frightened.[70]

✡ No Reward for Bravery ✡

Yitzhak Herz was in the small town of Dinslaken where the Jewish men were also rounded up. "I learned very soon from a policeman, who in his heart was still an anti-Nazi, that most of the Jewish men had been beaten up by members of the SA before being transported to Dachau. They were kicked, slapped in the face, and subjected to all sorts of humiliation. Many of those exposed to this type of ill-treatment had served in the German army during World War I. One of them, a Mr. Hugo B. C., had once worn with pride the Iron Cross First Class (the German equivalent of the Victoria Cross), which he had been awarded for bravery."[71]

✡ Saved by a Map ✡

Gerd Bochian lived next door to a religious seminary run by Rabbi Kupferstoch. The rabbi had been a hero during World War I and had been honored for his contribution of an important map before a crucial battle. He was said to have a protective letter signed by Hitler. When members of the SA showed up at the building, two German policemen standing guard sent them away. Fifteen-year-old Bochian believed that this action saved the building in which his family lived at that time.[72]

✡ A Loyal German ✡

They took Alfred Kleeman's father from his home in Gaukonigsho-ken to a nearby prison, about three or four kilometers away, in a city called Oxenford. This is where, Kleeman said, they were assembling all the Jews. "My mother was very courageous at that time. She went to this prison, and she somehow produced medals, an Iron Cross and some other certification that my father had earned as a soldier in the Kaiser's army in World War I. And she proved to whomever the authorities were at that time that he was certainly a loyal German, having fought in the Kaiser's army, and he was wounded once or twice. On the strength of that, they did let him come home."[73]

✡ I Served the Kaiser ✡

In Vienna 12-year-old Lucie Draschler was sent home from school early. "Suddenly we heard loud noises in the building, shouting, the trampling of heavy boots and finally the dreaded knock on the door. Four armed stormtroopers burst in and fell upon my father, beating him and pushing him down the stairs. Two of them followed him, while the other two told my grandfather to come with them. Then the most amazing thing happened, my grandfather stood before them and refused to go, he told them that he was an old man, that he had served his Kaiser in the Great War, and that he would not leave his home. They could easily have taken him, he was quite frail, but strangely enough they turned on their heels and left without a word."[74]

CHAPTER 4

Good-bye Daddy

Many of the survivors were young children during Kristallnacht, and their most vivid and horrifying memories are associated with their fathers disappearing or being arrested and seeing how their mothers reacted to the mistreatment of their spouses.

✡ Tearing Her Hair Out ✡

Ernest Kopstein was nine years old, living in Vienna on Kristallnacht. "I remember they knocked on the door very early in the morning; it might have been five, six o'clock in the morning, and I remember we were all still in bed. The night before I remember there was some rumor that things were going to happen, and I remember that my parents shoved some furniture in front of the door. They wanted to make it difficult for somebody to get into the apartment, and I was somewhat scared but I went to sleep that night.

"I woke the next morning to very loud banging on the door, and I remember my parents quickly getting up and just not doing anything to open the door, but being scared in the apartment. And I heard yelling on the outside, some men saying, 'Open up,' and eventually I heard a loud noise, which turned out to be them breaking down the door. They broke the door and pushed the furniture aside to get in, and I remember seeing a man with a pistol in his hand, and one or two other men with him, and they told my father to get dressed, that they would take him along. My father had to quickly get dressed, while my mother and my sister and I were standing there. It was a very dramatic scene.

"I remember they took my father away and my mother was just completely out of herself. She was crying and screaming and yelling. It's the only time I remember seeing her actually tear her hair out, literally tear her hair out, she was so upset by this. I remember that on the same day, my mother did not want to come back to the apartment, and she took us to stay overnight with some friends. I remember going to some friends or relatives and we stayed overnight elsewhere, and then I remember coming back home, I don't know how much later, maybe a couple of days later, and I remember my mother remarking that things were missing from the apartment."[75]

✡ You Cannot Take My Father ✡

Esther Gever also lived in Vienna. She was only eight years old when the Nazis came to her house. "They came from apartment to apartment knocking on the doors and pulling out the men. You couldn't object. If you did they beat you. They were brutal. They came for my father. I held his arm and . . . said, 'No, you cannot take my father.' I said, 'Why would you take my father, why?' I said, 'You will not take him. I will not let him go. He did not do anything.'

"At that point, one of the men grabbed me and threw me against the wall and I blacked out. I had a concussion. When I came to, my father was gone. My mother and my grandmother were standing near me. She was holding my baby sister in her arms. Our world collapsed completely. We had no choice. We weren't alone, but the pain was just unbearable. Where did they take him? We didn't know. Three weeks we didn't know where. After three weeks we were told he was in Dachau. We received the first postcard. It didn't tell us anything, because everything was censored so certain sentences were blacked out, only that he is well and he misses us and he loves us. Knocks on the door still terrify me."[76]

✡ No More Waiting ✡

George Jackson was a month from his seventh birthday. "I was in the Jewish school, and I remember around mid-morning a couple of mothers arrived to take their children home. We were not told anything. And then a couple of more mothers arrived and took their children home, and then our teacher disappeared, a male teacher. That was the day they arrested all, or tried to arrest all of the Jewish men of Vienna. My father was arrested. Eventually my mother came and got me out of school and I remember we went to two of the prisons we knew of to see if that is where he had been taken. We couldn't find out anything.

"There were also attacks on Jewish stores. Windows were smashed, books were burned out on the street. There were big mounds of books. I imagine not just Jewish books but anything objectionable to the Nazis was taken out and burned on the streets. Eventually we went home. We had not been able to locate my father, but late that day, he came back because they had, in a sense, over-arrested. They did not have enough jail cells for everybody and so they let quite a few people go at the end of that day.

"He was angry. He didn't really talk about his own personal experience that much, but I do remember his anger at what had happened. In a sense, he had expected something of that sort. He had wanted to get out long before the annexation, but he certainly tried to intensify our efforts for leaving as soon as possible, and I think at that point determined they were going to send me out by children's transport and not have me wait for my parents to exit." [77]

✡ It's Raining ✡

"I was 13 and a half. My father said something terrible is going to happen," Charles Heimler recalled of his childhood in Vienna. Heimler said his father had worked for a bank that had to get rid of its Jewish employees and he had been out of work for six months. He had been trying to get the family out of Austria. "That morning he rushed out to get a newspaper. While he was gone he got a telephone call that he shouldn't go out of the house, it's raining out of the house. That was the signal he shouldn't go out. Unfortunately, my father went down the steps of the apartment house and the Gestapo came to get one of the tenants who had a big store and the Gestapo ran into my father. They asked if he was a Jew. He was still in his night clothes and they said, 'Then you might as well come with us too.'

"I remember spending the next few days standing in endless lines with my mother at Gestapo headquarters and different places to find out what happened to my father. We heard a lot of people had been taken away. We stood in lines for hours and finally found out days later he was sent to Dachau."[78]

✡ The Nazi Idea of Fun ✡

"My brother and I stayed home," recalled Leo Glueckselig of Vienna. "There was no escape. Anyone caught on the street disappeared right away. You heard these terrible explosions. The Polish synagogue was one and a half blocks away when it blew up. You heard it and very quickly you knew what it was. Very few people were on the streets. But they came to the houses too that afternoon of deadly fear. My brother and I sat down because we couldn't bear it anymore and played cards. We heard over the radio that Göring said the action was over about 5 or 5:30. The bell rings and there are Nazis standing outside. My mother said, 'Göring said it was over,' but they took my father, brother and me. My mother stayed home alone and didn't know where we went. We were in prison. The police had an embarrassed look and they didn't touch us, only the SR [*sic*]. They opened a cell where drunks would sleep it off. They pressed about 100 people in there [gestures they were crushed together]. After two hours they took us in big police vans to the central police station in Vienna and brought us in the basement. There all hell broke loose. There was SS from Thuringia. They found out there was a father and son. A high officer said, 'Let's have some fun,' and told the son to slap his father. He refused. They grabbed the father and said, 'If he doesn't beat you up, we'll kill him.' So this father starts screaming at his son, calling him names, saying, 'Don't be so stubborn. If I tell you do it, hit me.' Finally the son started to cry and hit his father. Then they called it off."[79]

✡ A Nice Coat ✡

Fritzi Bellamy remembered Kristallnacht in Vienna as a day of rampant destruction. She left in the morning to go to a private studio where she studied arts and crafts and hat design. When she got to the class, another woman told her the coat she was wearing was so beautiful she wanted to borrow it for a fashion show. "I took off my coat and gave it to her. When I was ready to go home I didn't think anything of it and I put the coat on. I was walking toward my home and all of a sudden I see that people are staring at me who know me casually and are not saying anything. So I'm looking down at myself and I'm wearing a Nazi swastika insignia that she had pinned on my coat while she was at this fashion show and there I was walking home wearing this and it could have landed me in prison. I really didn't know what was going on yet because the streets I passed didn't have any signs of destruction yet. So I immediately tore this off and came home. As I approached my house, I saw fire burning further down in the distance and I realized it was the Parnishe temple which was at the end of the street adjoining ours. I got upstairs to mother and the radio was on and of course we realized a disaster was striking. Nobody came to our apartment. When dad didn't come home that night we knew something had happened. We didn't find out until about 10 days later through the Gestapo that my father was a prisoner in Dachau."[80]

✡ Playing the Wrong Cards ✡

Harry Katz was only five years old, but still remembers his apartment in Berlin. "I remember that morning hearing the sounds of the boots on the stairway coming up and I don't know whether I was afraid myself or whether I sensed the fear in the rest of the family, but there was a knock on the door and they gave us one hour to leave. My father wasn't home at the time, which was probably a good thing because they told my mother to find him and tell him not to come back because if he did they would have to pick him up. So she went out and found him and he didn't come back, and he wasn't picked up for that reason.

"I think the one reason why they were somewhat kind to us was because my father played cards with some of the SS and some of the local police and I guess that made them treat us a little bit better. They locked up our apartment so it couldn't be looted and told us if and when we found another apartment to come back and they would allow us to take our belongings.

"I think, on the other hand, the fact that my father knew some of the police and some of the SS probably gave us, or gave him, a false sense of security that no matter what happened we would be okay and we wouldn't have to leave as so many of our relatives and other friends had already left. And that turned out to be wrong."[81]

✡ Where's Father? ✡

Henry Warner Laurant and his family went into hiding. "We had some advance warning. Somehow there was a very effective grapevine in Berlin, and Jewish circles got wind of what was going to happen. Besides we didn't even have to get wind of it, the way in which the press painted and covered this incident, the assassination, the murder of vom Rath, by Grynszpan, was enough to make you pretty sure that something was going to come that was not pleasant. . . . My mother, my sister, and I went to the house of friends of ours, not far from our house we were living in then, in Berlin, and hid out there. We had no idea where my father was. He was with friends, but he didn't want us to know in case we were questioned in forceful ways, and so we didn't know where he was. We saw each other again at our house about four days later."[82]

✡ A Lucky Birth Date ✡

Max Kopfstein was 13 years old when the Gestapo came to his family's Berlin home looking for his father. He was not home, so they told his mother to call him to return home. While they were waiting, the Nazis asked how old the father was. "Mother replied, whether intentionally or not I don't know, by giving the year of his birth—'85—instead of his age, then 53. They misunderstood, thinking he was 85 years old, and exclaimed, 'What, so old?' whereupon they left."[83]

✡ Father Is Missing ✡

Herman Cohn lived in Gelsenkirchen in the northern part of the Ruhr area of Germany. He was not home when the pogrom began but received a call from his stepmother telling him to come home immediately. She said his father was missing and that the SS had broken into their house that morning.

"I took the first train. My father was missing. He had received a call from his brother during the night that the Nazis had invaded his home and had set the furniture store on fire. The place was surrounded by SS. He went back to the car, a brand new Mercedes. The SS spotted him. One knew him and said, 'There goes the Jew's brother.' He ran into a nursery and there was a pit in the back where they accumulated leaves that they turned into fertilizer. He stayed in that pit until sunup. He heard SS and dogs looking for him. There was enough moisture for him to breath. At dawn he came out of the leaves and looked for his car, but it was gone. So he took a train home. We lived on a street with an incline. As he was coming up, the SS spotted him and beat him to a pulp. We didn't know. I came home in the afternoon and he was missing. The next day we heard he was in a hospital in Essen."[84]

✡ Shipped to Dachau ✡

Joel Darmstadter was only a few weeks from celebrating his 10th birthday when life in Mannheim "took a quantum change for the worst." He recalled being confused by what happened on Kristallnacht. "A bunch of hooligan Nazis or Nazi sympathizers came to our house and destroyed most of the furniture by sawing and hacking it to pieces and throwing the books out the window where they were burned. My grandfather, my parents, my brother and I were cowering while this was taking place. Topping it all off was the arrest of my father the next morning. He was shipped off to Dachau. I was bewildered by what was going on. Some people's homes had been utterly destroyed and some people moved in with each other. I think the local cantor stayed with us for a few days."[85]

✡ Everything Is Gone ✡

On Kristallnacht, 11-year-old Lisleotte Foster saw her father cry for the first time. "He went into the shop in the morning and came back and he said, 'Everything is gone. What they didn't destroy they carried out.' I see my mom standing there saying, 'Everything will be ok.' My dad was so upset. It was the first time I saw him cry. I didn't know why they would do that. It didn't make any sense to me. They tried to explain it to me over and over and I couldn't understand. I'm a Jew. I don't look any different than the next person. I could never understand that. I felt so bad for my dad. Our life changed after that completely. He had to work for somebody else. The money was confiscated. Whatever money there was. He got a certain salary and that was it. We had a certain allotment each month. It was too much to die and too little to live. Then you couldn't have any electrical appliances, no radios, even pets were taken away. Everything you lived with all your life was completely changed."[86]

✡ One Shoe ✡

Eric Friedmann lived in Erfurt, the capital today of the state of Thuringia, and had not experienced any anti-Semitism before Kristallnacht. "I was 8 going on 9. I remember very distinctly our wonderful Erfurt police coming to take my father to Buchenwald concentration camp very early in the morning. It was still dark. In the dark, he was groping for his sandals. One had got kicked in and they didn't give him time to find another shoe before they took him away to a concentration camp. That is when I began to experience anti-Semitism."[87]

✡ The Letter ✡

In the peaceful town of Ulm, which sits along the Danube, and was the birthplace of Albert Einstein, 12-year-old Gabriele Gatzert remembered her father wasn't allowed to go out at night. "I remember being in my room with my parents. . . . My father was expecting a letter about the business and he was waiting for that letter to come. The doorbell rang at two in the morning and he went downstairs in his slippers and his pajamas and he thought that was the letter. It wasn't. It was the SS or SR [*sic*]. Some very young men picked him up. He asked if he could take clothes and they wouldn't allow it. I woke up. Our living room had a very small window where my father's chair was, where he would read the paper. I looked out and I could see my father leave. I heard the next day the synagogue was burned down and I couldn't go to school. My mother went to see my father in a prison and I think she brought him some food and clothes. He was all bloody and he said he had fallen the night before. That wasn't true at all. He didn't dare talk. After they picked him up, they took him to the police court where there was a fountain and they threw him in, showered him with really cold water and then they had all the men jump like frogs. That was before they sent him to Dachau.

"The man who was supposed to send the letter went to Dachau to press my father to give away his business to the Nazis. Of course, he had no choice but to do that. He also signed that he would leave Germany in six weeks."[88]

✡ Cleaning Up ✡

Av Perlmutter was an 11-year-old living in Vienna when the violence began. "I saw some elderly Jews who were given toothbrushes and they were asked to clean the streets of anti-Nazi signs which were left from the prior election. They were surrounded by cheering non-Jews and, for all I know, even their neighbors.

"My neighbor was asked by my parents to go and get me. The lady was gracious enough to come and find me. I was actually a couple of streets away. She brought me back and just when I came back, I happened to see the Germans had just gotten into our house. My uncle Ze'ev Gottlieb had lived in an apartment above us. They dragged him out and they dragged my father out and they beat them up on the streets. I remember my sister running after him crying and they beat her up as well."[89]

✡ No More Credit ✡

Sabina Katz remembered that her father used to give people credit in his store. "When they banged on the door with their fists at 6 o'clock in the morning on that fateful day, when they came to arrest my father, they apologized because there wasn't one who didn't owe my father money at that time, when they came to arrest him. They came in the morning to arrest all the men and parade them through the city, beat them up. My father was not beaten up. I don't know why. But they sent him to Dachau."[90]

✡ It'll Blow Over ✡

Fourteen-year-old Stephanie Robertson lived in Dresden, the capital today of the German state of Saxony. Robertson's father had apparently been taken during the night, and she didn't know he was gone until she woke up. Later, she learned he'd been taken to Buchenwald. "I really didn't realize the full horror of it. I had been sheltered. All of a sudden, my father had disappeared. And my mother was crying. And the synagogues were burnt down, and windows smashed. But I wasn't allowed to go outside. So I was put in the playroom with some nice books and told, 'Don't go out' and 'Here's some nice books for you near the box of sweets' and 'It'll blow over.' That sort of thing. I didn't realize the horror of it."[91]

✡ Like a Lion ✡

Jutta Rose lived in Hanover in northern Germany. She saw SA men come into her house on the morning of Kristallnacht. They rang the bell, and she thought the maid must have answered. "They just pushed her aside and stormed into the house. 'Where's the *Juden?*'

"They threw my father down the stairs. Blood was all over. My mother was like a lion. I had never seen her like this. She said, 'You don't dare to touch anything in this house! I am a Christian woman and you get out of here!' She was the kindest and best person you can imagine. They put the things back. They did. My father was downstairs bleeding and was taken away. I was hanging onto my mother. I was afraid because I thought they would take my mother and me, too. But they left with my father. We were frightened stiff because we didn't know what happened or if we would ever see my father again.

"My father was taken to Buchenwald. We didn't even know that concentration camps were there. Before, it wasn't known; they built them all behind the scenes. They were building it for labor because Hitler wanted to make a war against all Europe."[92]

✡ God Is with Us ✡

Armin Kern learned that all the synagogues in Germany were set afire on Kristallnacht, including the synagogue in his hometown of Landau, which was known as a cultural center surrounded by vineyards. "This upset us greatly. It was not a good sign burning the house of God. What would happen next? Later in the morning we heard on the radio that the German people were upset with the murder of vom Rath; the synagogues were burned out of revenge.

"Later, we saw a mob of men coming towards the house carrying all sorts of tools. The doorbell rang and they came in demanding, 'We are looking for weapons.' My father answered that we didn't have any weapons. They shouted back, 'Get out.' 'Oh my god,' said my father, and one of them answered, 'God is with us now, no longer with you.'

"We went outside in the yard. Other gentiles stood around. They just looked at us never saying a word. It was a moment that I have never forgotten. I decided at that moment that I did not want anything to do with Germany anymore. Any love for the country that I might have still had was now gone."

The mob eventually left. Armin's home was a shambles. "They had wrecked the furniture. Dishes, glass and ornaments were broken. Cognac was splashed against the walls. I remembered the smell for years. Our typewriter and radio were gone. The curtains were not touched, belying the appearance from the outside.

"Later in the afternoon my father was arrested and taken to the Jewish community center with all the other Jewish men from Landau and surrounding villages. I was lucky. Had I been 16, I would have also been arrested.

"We had no idea where my father was. All the men spent the night in the center being questioned by the Gestapo and some were forced on the spot to sign over properties and bank accounts to the Nazi party."

The day after Kristallnacht Armin was on a train and got involved in a conversation with a young Aryan man about what had happened the previous day. "His comment was, 'You knew for the past five years that you were no longer wanted, why did you not leave before?' I have never forgotten this conversation; it was the voice of the German people."

Armin's mother spoke to the Gestapo and was told her husband and all the other Jewish men from Landau had been transported to Dachau. "My mother explained to the Gestapo that my father was a veteran of World War I and we have our affidavit at the American Consulate and were waiting for our quota number 6134 to be called. We needed him as we all had to go together to the consulate. The Gestapo urged my mother to write a letter to headquarters, telling the story. In the meantime, my father wrote that he was well and he needed money to buy extra food. The money was sent via money order. After about four weeks, he was released from Dachau and joined us in Bruchsal."[93]

✡ A Frightful Day ✡

Kurt Ladner was a child in Austria. The day began like any other. "Kristallnacht my father and brother left for work early in the morning. My brother Fritz and I left together, they to work, and I to school. I was in class only one hour when the school was dismissed, and we were told to go home and to stay home and not to loiter in the street. On my way home, I saw a lot of activity going on. SA men, Hitler Youth and the police were scrambling and assembling on all major street corners.

"When I got home my mother explained to me what and how serious the situation for Jews was. She explained that a Jewish man named Grynszpan assassinated a German diplomat in France. Reprisals against Jews had already started in Germany and were about to begin in Austria. Just then we heard a band of SA men marching and singing about drowning the Jews in the ocean. My neighbor and friend, Sigi Hudes, came running to tell me that the windows in the Klucki Temple were being shattered and that Jews were being arrested in the streets. At this news, my mother paled, worried about my father and brothers. She looked at me, then pulled me close to her and kissed me, for she had made up her mind to send me to warn my father and brother, Hans. I am sure she did not make this decision lightly, but she figured a little boy dressed in a lederhosen and a Tyrolian jacket might be safe and worth the risk. She told me where to go and tell my father to take the shortest route home, or go to the nearest aunt. I was just about to run out of the apartment, when she said to me, 'You come home by yourself, not with your father.'

"As I jogged up Wallenstein Strasse, I looked towards the Klucki Temple and saw Jews being hoarded and hit with night sticks. I also saw smoke near the Temple (we found out later that they burned all the Jewish scrolls and later the building inside). I ran by the Klucki street rather fast. What I saw was very limited, but enough to make me very scared. Also, I was hoping that nobody would recognize me on the street. I saw people assembled, so I crossed the street and the 'Friedens Brucke' into the Ninth District to my father's job. When I got there, I was told that my father and brother had left about twenty minutes ago.

"I then went to the house of my two aunts, but my father was not there. I warned them not to leave their apartment, and at full speed, I ran home. I reported to my mother what I had seen in the Klucki

Gasse and that my father and brother had left before I got there. My mother walked up and down, from the kitchen to the bedroom window, back and forth. She finally asked me if I had had any problems in the street or if anyone attempted to stop me. I replied, 'No. I ran most of the way and when I saw a few people standing, I crossed the street.'

"She nodded with a faint smile and said, 'Could you run to Fritz's school and tell him to come home?'

"I said, 'I'll run the other way, so I won't pass the Klucki Temple.'

"I put my jacket back on and ran down the stairs. His school was known as a Jewish retraining place by the Nazis. It would have been easy for them to grab a whole bunch of Jews in one swoop. I had just reached the first floor, when I saw my brother Fritz coming up. He grabbed me around my waist and picked me up, demanding to know where I was going. On the way up, I told him that I was on the way to warn him to come home. I also said that my father and brother were still not at home. When we both walked in, my mother hugged us, and Fritz said to my mother, 'It is very risky to walk in the street' and that the only thing we could do now was wait and hope that my father and brother would be home soon.

"We sat around and waited and waited and, for the first time, I listened to my mother thinking out loud and I got really scared. She painted the worst scenario of what could have happened to my father. Our neighbors, the Hudes, came over and told us that they jailed Jews and held them in the Karajan Gasse School. They also told us of cruelty and beatings. Many things we heard and were told we hoped were only rumors, but everything turned out to be the sad truth.

"It was not until late in the afternoon when my father and brother walked in. My mother immediately started to scold them, and to ask questions. 'Why had they not come home earlier?' As my mother was talking, you could see under what tension she was under and how relieved she looked when they walked in. My father said that they went to another job in the Second District. They were dressed in dirty painting clothing, carrying ladders and bags of brushes. They actually passed the SS and SA men and groups of Austrians that assisted the SS in capturing Jews, but no one ever looked at them or stopped them. On their way home, they saw the Leopolds Temple being destroyed and Jewish men hoarded together. But, my father said, 'We kept on walking and thankfully got home.'

"It was a frightful day. We were sitting around, afraid to go near the window, wondering if the Nazis would come to homes and apartments to arrest Jews. We were up most of the night not knowing if relatives and friends had been arrested. None of us had telephones and our communications with our relatives was through visits.

"It took a few days for this episode to calm down and Jews slowly started to emerge from their houses. We learned that two of my cousins and several friends of my parents and brothers had been arrested. It took weeks before we heard from my cousins, Karl and Hanel. One sent a postcard from Dachau and the other from Buchenwald. The entire extended family was scrambling to obtain exit visas for our cousins. At that time, if you could show to the authorities that an exit visa to any foreign country existed, the prisoners would be released and ordered to leave the country within the shortest period of time. For money, and I mean lots of money, their families were able to acquire visas to Shanghai, China and one to Yugoslavia. After a few weeks, they were released from their imprisonment. Once at home, they were depressed and totally silent. If they should reveal what took place in these concentration camps, they would be arrested again. In fear of that threat, they did not speak at all. They left Austria just in the nick of time because a short time later, all releases were cancelled."[94]

✡ Embarrassed and Ashamed ✡

Golly D. was 16 years old and lived in the large port city of Bremen. "We were fast asleep. I and my family, the four of us fast asleep when we heard pounding on the front door. Heavy pounding. My father quickly went down the steps, opened the door, and there were two Brown[shirt] Nazi troopers standing there. 'Tell your family to get dressed quickly and come with us. Come along!'

"We had no choice. We quickly got dressed and the two troopers delivered us to a mess hall which was in the center of town. And, as we entered, realized that all the other Jews from the city had also been rounded up and also been brought to this mess hall. Nobody knew why. Nobody knew what was going to happen. They let us sit there for hours on end, hour after hour after hour, until finally they separated the women from the men and the men were taken away . . . and so was my father and my brother.

"In the morning, my mother and I and all women were allowed to return home. And that's when we found out what had been happening during the night while we were gathered together there in the mess hall. That the Brownshirts were busy smashing the Jewish store windows, entering the Jewish homes and apartments, smashing everything that they could. My father's business was destroyed that night. And of course we had one synagogue in Bremen, which was burned down."

The next day Golly went to school as though nothing had happened. As she walked to her classroom, her homeroom teacher came down the steps and looked at her sadly and said, 'Miss Golly, I'm awfully sorry, but Jews are no longer to attend school.' So, I had no choice but to turn back. And I walked home with my head down, and I realized that my plans for the future had been shattered."

The following day one of her non-Jewish classmates came to visit. At that point it was taboo to have any social contact with Jews. "Now this pure Aryan classmate of mine, coming from a very prominent family—her father was the most prominent lawyer in Bremen—came to our house, came upstairs, and she said she only came with one message. In the name of her family, she wanted to express how terribly embarrassed and ashamed they were about what had happened the previous night, the Kristallnacht. And I could never forget this gesture and I'm still in contact. I'm still corresponding with her. And whenever I go home to Bremen, we do get together."[95]

✡ Hide Your Eyes ✡

Hannele Zürndorfer lived in a district in Düsseldorf and learned after Kristallnacht that a gang of Brownshirts had been imported to rid the area of Jews and had been instructed exactly where to go. Hannele said a neighbor who lived across the hall was not bothered because the Nazis obviously knew he was not a Jew. The neighbor would later say he was "ashamed to be German," but did nothing while a horde of men rampaged through the Zürndorfers' apartment. Hannele saw her father standing in his nightshirt trying to prevent the men from destroying a valuable painting and then watching helplessly as one shredded it with a knife. As she huddled with her mother and sister in her parents' bed, one Nazi whispered to them, "Children don't look, don't look children. Hide your eyes. I am sorry. I had to do it."

The rabble left the apartment in ruins, but the family was happy to be alive. Hannele said she can't remember what she thought or did at the time, but had some specific images in her mind. "The most vivid, because to me it was the most shattering, is of my father slumped on a chair that had been overlooked in the kitchen beside the cooker, weeping quite shamelessly. My heart turned over and seemed to stop. Never in my whole life had I seen my father weep."[96]

✡ Escape to the Forest ✡

Johanna Neumann was a few weeks from her eighth birthday when she started out for school in Hamburg. "Going to school I passed our synagogue, and what I saw were hordes of people standing in front of the synagogue and throwing stones into the beautiful stained glass windows. These are not the days of mass media, mass information, radio, television or anything like that, so we really didn't know what happened during the night. We arrived in school and the teachers immediately told us what had happened. I don't remember the exact words she used to explain what happened but she said that something terrible had happened and that our parents had all been informed. We should sit in class quietly and that we would be picked up shortly."

Johanna's mother picked her up from school and took her to her grandmother's home. Her father had gone downtown. When he returned, he described how the Jewish stores had been vandalized. She said she could visualize the destruction: "Clothing, fur coats, perfume, ink, everything was thrown into the streets, mixed in with the broken glass from the windows of these huge department stores." Her father said if the Nazis saw a Jew, they snatched him and put him in the type of car used to transport criminals to prison.

Despite the danger and uncertainty, Johanna's father insisted they return to their home, but they kept the lights off so it would appear no one was home. When people started knocking on their door in the middle of the night, they ignored it and whoever had come went away. The next morning Johanna's family returned to her grandmother's home. They figured that since her grandfather had died, the Germans wouldn't come to the house since they were only interested in arresting men. Several other friends and family members also gathered in her grandmother's apartment. "The SS came twice and asked my grandmother where my grandfather was and, each time she said he had passed away in '35, and they left again. But at that point it had become really too dangerous because the next time they came they may really want to search the apartment and find the men. So that night, perhaps the second or third night into the whole pogrom, the three men left and went to a place called Blankenese, which is a summer resort. It has a little forest and a Jewish summer camp. A number of Jewish families from Hamburg had escaped to that place because all day long they would stay in the forest and hide there, and so did my father and these other two gentlemen. And they stayed there until the end of the Kristallnacht. So they were not taken."[97]

✡ My Father's Ashes ✡

Ursula Rosenfeld was just 13 years old when the Nazis arrested her father. She had eaten dinner with him the night before Kristallnacht, not knowing it was the last meal she'd ever have with him. The next morning, after she returned from school, Ursula learned her father had been taken by the police. Later, she would learn what happened from survivors of Buchenwald. When the Jews arrived, their braces and shoelaces were taken away. "My father was quite an outspoken person . . . and he protested and said, 'You can't treat these old people like this.' So they made an example of him and they beat him to death in front of everybody in order to instill terror and obedience. We heard a few days later that he had died of a heart attack, but this was the story the Nazis told all the families of the people they killed. . . . The Nazis offered us my father's ashes in return for money. Eventually the urn came and we buried it in the Jewish cemetery. But, of course, whether it was his ashes one never knows."[98]

CHAPTER 5

Walking Through the Looking Glass

One of the most frightening aspects of Kristallnacht was the uncertainty about what was happening, where the incidents fit into the larger picture of life in Germany. Worse still was the anxiety associated with not knowing what the Nazis were going to do after people were seized from their homes. Some believed they were going to be killed, others were loaded on trains or buses with no idea what lay at the end of the journey. Even upon arriving at a final destination, which for thousands of men was a concentration camp, few had any inkling what treatment to expect, as little was known in 1938 about what was taking place in these prisons. Women and children were not sent to camps, and some of the men evaded capture. Virtually all of them, however, had nightmarish experiences they could never forget.

✡ Shoot My Child First ✡

Hertha Nathorff was a gynecologist in Berlin. She was married to a doctor who was out making house calls on November 10 as Nazis were rampaging through the streets' of Berlin. He returned home to tell Hertha that a police action appeared to be under way and that a number of his patients had been arrested. Many, he said, had been taken during a wedding, and now he was responding to calls from men and women who were suffering heart attacks after seeing their loved ones taken away by the Gestapo. Against her wishes, Hertha's husband went back out to see more patients.

At 9:30 that night, Hertha was in the apartment when the doorbell rang and she asked who was there. It was the police demanding to be let inside. "Trembling, I open the door, knowing what they want.

"'Where is Herr Doctor?'

"'He's not home,' I say.

"'What do you mean? The porter's wife says she saw him come home.'

"'He was here, but he was called out again.'

"They go toward the first door. Locked. The second door. Locked.

"'These are our offices where we see patients,' I explain. 'Ever since we were robbed, I always lock them in the evening when I'm here alone.'

"They go to the next door. 'Please don't shake it,' I say. 'My child is sleeping in there.'

"'We know that Jewish trick.' And, holding a revolver under my nose, one of them says, 'Another word and a bullet will be in your brain. Where have you hidden your husband?'

"My knees are shaking. Just stay calm, stay calm, I tell myself. 'I'm not lying. My husband isn't at home. But shoot my child first, then me. And don't miss.'

"I open the door to the bedroom of my sleeping child. The two young policemen are already preparing to leave. Finally they seem to believe me. But in this instant I hear someone opening the door of our apartment. My husband comes in. Unlucky soul—he arrives at the very moment I think he has been saved. And just as he stands there, they take him away.

"'You can thank God your wife doesn't have a bullet in her head.'

"The young kid dares to repeat this, and he dares to use the name of God. And they leave with my husband. I run out onto the street after them. 'Where are you going with my husband, what's happening to him?'

"They shove me away, brutally. 'Tomorrow morning, at Alexander Square, you can ask for him.'

"I watch how they climb into a car and drive off into the night with my husband."[99]

✡ The Home of Goethe ✡

Hans Berger was arrested in Wiesbaden. "At about six o'clock on Sunday morning the train stopped at the station in Weimar, Goethe's city, which for all times will remain most horribly linked in my memory with the following scene in the tunnel between the platforms. We had to get off the train by compartments, and had to run, on the double, accompanied by blows with steel rods and pokes by rifle butts, along the platform, down the stairs, into the tunnel. Woe unto him who tripped or fell down the stairs. The very least was that the ones coming after him had to trample over him, or also fell down and were brought back onto their feet by renewed blows and jabs.

"In the tunnel itself we had to place ourselves in lines of ten, one behind the other, the first person with his face directly against the wall, and the gendarmes saw to it that we stood crammed together like herrings. The poor people who stood last in the line had to suffer blows and pokes, the effect of which was that the lines pressed closer and closer together. I was standing in the middle; in the end it was hardly possible to breathe. On top of it, whips whistled above our bare heads and the most obscene bellowing and most vile phrases that anyone can imagine poured forth onto the desperate crowd of packed in Jews. This lasted two hours. Then, by rows and once again on the double, we had to run further through the tunnel, up the steps, and climb onto waiting trucks, which were equipped with seats, constantly under blows from whips and sticks that were part of all this.

"In the cars we were told: 'Put on your hats and lower your heads!' Woe unto him who did not duck low enough. A blow to his head with the whip or a stick was the least he could expect. Off we went at terrible speed through the forest. After approximately a ten minute drive the car stopped. Once again, on the double, we got out and ran through a gate into a big yard, in which thousands of fellow sufferers were standing lined up in rows of ten. We were in the Buchenwald concentration camp."[100]

✡ We Didn't Know Where We Were Going ✡

Fred Marcus met all the important people of Breslau in a courtyard where they all watched the synagogue burning. "It was [an] important place for Jews. There was a seminary and many famous rabbis were educated there. I saw the rabbis, the lawyers, everybody was there [in the courtyard]. I was there in the morning and they kept bringing people in all day long. All of a sudden, we were told we were going somewhere and were taken to the main railroad station. That was one of the worst things. People were spitting at us and throwing tomatoes at us. SR [*sic*] men had guns and they were nasty. We were loaded on railroad cars. We didn't know where we were going." Marcus ended up in Buchenwald.[101]

✡ Scream as Loud as You Can ✡

Dr. Harry Stern was the president of the local lodge of B'nai B'rith in Erfurt. He was taken to a gymnasium and then hauled into a restroom where two SA men were waiting with truncheons. "One of them raised his club and touched me with it. The other said, 'Scream as loud as you can,' which I did. They evidently wanted to circumvent the order they had been given to beat us. Then I was shoved out of the washroom and grabbed by other SA men and made to stand with my face to the wall. . . . They forced us to walk with bended knees, the worst torture I have endured. . . . Some of the Nazis singled out Jews they knew personally in order to vent their anger on them. The lawyer Flesch, who was a baptized Christian, was tormented and insulted especially by an SA man whose wife he had represented in court in a divorce case. A number of Jews—irrespective of age and physical constitution—were forced to climb up the ladders mounted in the gym. Nazis stood at their bases, wielding riding whips, and struck out at their victims on the ladders as long as they remained in reach. . . . We had to stand in formation and march around to the tune of the 'Horst Wessel Song.' Then the command was given to shout '*Juda verrecke!*' [Judah perish!], which we were *compelled* to do. After that we were loaded onto buses and transported to Buchenwald, where we arrived at dawn."[102]

✡ An Unforgettable Performance ✡

Lorraine Allard remembered being awakened at 2 a.m. by the sound of banging. Two uniformed Nazis shouted that her family was under arrest and to put clothes on and accompany them. "I remember it was a very cold, very dark night, and we all went off to an assembly point, which was like a big square. And there were just thousands of other Jews, and I mean thousands. There were people I knew and people I didn't know, and people getting beaten up, and people crying. I think everyone was petrified. My main memory is of the cold, and the dark, and my brother crying. . . . I remember, also very vividly, that they were beating up the rabbi and he was bleeding. They had fetched the Torahs out of the synagogue. And I think they were trampling on them. . . . We were taken to a theater, and we sat there as if we were going to watch a performance. The performance was that they fetched the men out on the stage and made them jump over the chairs and over the tables. If they couldn't do it, they whipped them. It's a sight you don't forget, one of the worst I experienced."[103]

✡ A Bearded Jew ✡

Lisbeth Kornreich was 25 years old. She was walking down the street near her home in Vienna when she saw a group of 40 to 50 schoolchildren being led by a teacher. The group stopped in the middle of the block. Kornreich did not know that there was a small synagogue there until she witnessed people opening the doors and pulling out the seats and pews and Torahs. "They set them on fire. That's what they brought the children for, so the children could stand on the sidewalk, and see that in the front yard of that building, religious objects were being burned. When I saw this, I turned the other corner around the block and ran home."

Kornreich lived on the outskirts of town near the Vienna woods. Her parents owned a piece of property where they hoped to build a retirement home. At the time they had a little weekend house there. Kornreich was walking from where she lived to that house when she saw a bunch of hoodlums attacking an old bearded Jew. They were pulling his beard out so that blood ran over his chin, with the flesh. "This I'll never forget."[104]

✡ Don't Scream ✡

Fred Kort was 15 years old, working in a Jewish factory in Leipzig installing some electrical systems when the Gestapo came. "They arrested us, picked us up right from the job, and took us to the central square of Karlsruhe where the city hall and everything was located, all the governmental buildings. It was the capital of the province of Baden, and there was a mob by the thousands. We had to walk through that group of quote unquote mad people, and they beat us, made us bloody, and it was awful."

Fred was taken to a police horse barn and made to face the wall. Every few minutes a voice from a loudspeaker would say, "You don't have to cry, it will be just a few more minutes and we'll shoot you to death." Fred couldn't take it and began screaming. Someone poked him and told him not to scream. "Late that night, it must have been about 10 or 11, they picked out all the minors, including me, and sent them home. Maybe four or five hundred adult males were sent to Dachau. It was the first association we heard of Dachau."[105]

✡ Nobody Helped ✡

Alfred Kleeman was at home in a rooming house in Munich. "Three Gestapo agents came and they lined us all up. . . . They wanted anybody over 18 to step forward. We were mostly under 18, but there were three or four of us who were our leaders, and they were over 18, so they stepped forward and were taken away by the Gestapo. That day we did not know exactly what was happening, but, as it turned out, they were part of the tens of thousands who were taken to Dachau, a concentration camp very close to the city of Munich. Now the rest of us, we were told by whoever was left in the leadership, that they closed our vocational school and there was nothing else for us to do but to go home to our own cities or towns. So this is what we then did."

Alfred took a train to his home village of Gaukonigshoken. "When I finally got to my parents' house, I could see already from the outside, the main door was smashed. In this house everything had been turned upside down. All the closets, full of dishes, were just literally turned upside down. The food—they had canned food that was stored in a big closet—even that they destroyed. And the feather beds were cut and the feathers were flying all over. And all the furniture in the entire house was damaged with axes and there was . . . not even a single dish that was totally intact that we could find to eat from. Even our store, which was in the house, our textile store, which we were still running at that time I believe, even there, they went in and damaged much of the merchandise.

"There was little sympathy from the neighbors, even though I vaguely remember there was perhaps one Christian neighbor that did come over and bring us something to eat. But other than that, nobody offered to help, to begin to clean up."[106]

✡ What a Shame ✡

Ernest Heppner said there was an air of expectation before Kristallnacht, but no one knew what would happen. In the morning his father received a call from one of the workers to come to the factory because there was trouble and he left to close it up. "I was at home with the maid. My brother by that time was married and lived someplace else with his wife and a little baby. I heard some noise out front. We lived in a residential area in one of these big apartment buildings. Most middle class people, even the affluent ones, didn't own homes unless they had a villa. We lived on the second floor and I looked out and I saw a truck come up the street with SS troops and stop at one house.

I was watching them go in and come out a few minutes later with some of our Jewish neighbors and push them up in the truck. Next house, same thing. Then they came across to my house. I didn't wait for them. I ran to the back room, jumped out the window, got on my bike, got away.

"Then I was running around aimlessly for awhile and I was afraid of the road block and I got on the train, on a steam car, to see what was happening. 'Where am I going to go now, where am I going to hide?' So I got off. I wanted to see what was happening downtown. I was very adventuresome. That was my scouting nature. I did some crazy things. So I got on a street car and I could see the smoke from a distance already. I leaned out; I was standing on the platform. I could see smoke and came to the name of the place, I can't remember the name, and I saw the flames shooting out of the dome of the synagogue. I was just furious. That affected me more than perhaps anything else in all these years. But I remember next to me stood an old German woman and she muttered to herself, translated into English, 'Oh, what a shame. What a beautiful building that was.' Next to us stood a Nazi in civvies and not in uniform. He reached and pulled the cord, brought the train to a stop, yanked her out just for that remark."[107]

✡ Beyond Description ✡

Kurt Klein had left Germany in 1937 and was living in Buffalo when he received letters from his family about what had happened on Kristallnacht. His mother wrote: "'What happened on that night is really beyond description. I won't go into it here, but suffice to say that we all acquired a set of mini-furniture in a hurry,' meaning, of course, that they had come into the house and smashed all the furniture. We later found out from other relatives who left Germany after Kristallnacht that a gang of SA stormtroopers invaded my parents' home that night. They were led by a former classmate of mine who had been in and out of our home, who had eaten at our table, and at whose house I had spent some time. He lined up my elderly parents against the wall, and they all made very ominous threats toward them while they proceeded to vandalize the home and destroy most of my parents' belongings. They also arrested my father and hauled him off to the local jail. That was still better than what happened to most people. My father was already quite elderly by that time and perhaps that is the reason he was not sent to a concentration camp, but all the younger and middle-aged men were sent to concentration camps. We would get these letters subsequently in which my mother or father would say such and such a family still has no news from their husband or someone has now been reunited and we talked to them and they are okay. Eventually most of the men who had been arrested on Kristallnacht were in fact sent back home, but some never made it out of the concentration camp."[108]

✡ A Foul Exhibition ✡

Michael Bruce, a non-Jewish Englishman, provided this eyewitness account of Kristallnacht: "Hurriedly we went out into the street. It was crowded with people, all hurrying towards a nearby synagogue, shouting and gesticulating angrily. We followed. As we reached the synagogue and halted, silent and angry, on the fringe of the mob, flames began to rise from one end of the building. It was the signal for a wild cheer. The crowd surged forward and greedy hands tore seats and woodwork from the building to feed the flames.

"Behind us we heard more shouts. Turning, we saw a section of the mob start off along the road towards Israel's store where, during the day, piles of granite cubes, ostensibly for repairing the roads, had been heaped. Youths, men and women, howling deliriously, hurled the blocks through the windows and at the closed doors. In a few minutes the doors gave way and the mob, shouting and fighting, surged inside to pillage and loot.

"By now the streets were a chaos of screaming bloodthirsty people lusting for Jewish bodies. I saw Harrison of *The News Chronicle*, trying to protect an aged Jewess who had been dragged from her home by a gang. I pushed my way through to help him and, between us, we managed to heave her through the crowd to a side street and safety.

"We turned back towards Israel's, but now the crowd, eager for fresh conquests, was pouring down a side road towards the outskirts of the city. We hurried after them in time to see one of the foulest exhibitions of bestiality I have ever witnessed.

"The object of the mob's hate was a hospital for sick Jewish children, many of them cripples or consumptives. In minutes, the windows had been smashed and the doors forced. When we arrived, the swine were driving the wee mites out over the broken glass, barefooted and wearing nothing but their nightshirts. The nurses, doctors, and attendants were being kicked and beaten by the mob leaders, most of whom were women."[109]

✡ Treated with Care ✡

In his memoir Shlomo Samson recalled Kristallnacht in Leipzig. "On that day, the aroused mob forced its way into our flat. It was morning and all four of us were at home; grandmother, mother and two children. The vom Rath avengers were equipped with iron bars to demolish everything in sight. After a careful search ascertained that there were no men in the house, they contented themselves with smashing all crockery, glass and windowpanes and chopping up some furniture. Then they moved on to search for grander homes, which no doubt provided them with more gratification. In the center of town, all display windows in the many Jewish shops were shattered, but the main targets were the synagogues and the Jewish schools which were burnt down.

"After the 'hurricane' passed, we were very anxious about what might happen during the following nights. Above all, I was in danger of being arrested, so we decided not to sleep at home for a few nights. We slipped away to the homes of some of father's friends who were citizens of Argentina and Uruguay. The doors of their homes displayed foreign flags and coats of arms which somehow convinced the marauding mob to leave those homes untouched. In temporary sanctuary, we were able to sleep peacefully for a few nights before we returned to our own flat.

"Two or three days following Kristallnacht, when things had quieted down, I took a cautious walk through the city. Our Etz-Chaim Synagogue, a free-standing building, had been totally burned down. The big temple which bordered on residential buildings was ignited 'with care'—the shell was standing. Other synagogues, located in dwelling houses, such as the Keil Street Synagogue, were totally destroyed but not burned down. In this respect, the shtiebels [small houses or rooms used for communal prayer] fared best. They were small and unobtrusive and some were in back buildings, so that they were hard to find. I passed the school, which had been set aflame. Only the outside walls remained."[110]

✡ Ashamed to Be a German ✡

Selma Schiratzki was a teacher at the Rykestrasse School, a Jewish elementary school in Berlin. "I left the train at Hackescher Markt. In the Kleine Schönhauserstrasse, I passed a stationery shop in front of which a small group of people had gathered. The windows of the shop had been smashed and a school girl was bending down to pick up one of the scattered treasures. I flew at her: 'What? Stealing on top of it? Aren't you ashamed of yourself?' And one of the women in the crowd nodded approval: 'Yes, you are quite right.'

"When I arrived at the school we decided to carry on with the lessons for the moment and contact the school administration of the Jewish community to hear their decision. But already during the first lesson many excited mothers came to take their children home. While I was still speaking to them and had their children called from their classes, Baurat Schiller arrived at the school. He was a municipal official in charge of superintending the school building and the carrying out of any necessary repairs. Under the impact of the heart-rending scene, he said, 'One is ashamed to be a German.'

"The lessons were soon broken off that morning. In the afternoon I received, by telephone, the information that the 'people's wrath' had by now also poured itself out over our schoolhouse. The youths of the Chorinerstrasse—some 200 children—led by a number of grown-ups had broken into the building, smashed all the windows, opened the bookcase in the teachers' room by force and taken away a number of musical instruments."[111]

✡ Hippocratic Treatment ✡

At 4 a.m. on November 10 the SA broke into a Jewish hospital and examined each patient. Those who were able to walk were forced to leave the hospital and assembled in the town square. The men were later taken to a prison and ultimately to Dachau. The Jewish nurses who had also been forced to leave the hospital with the patients were allowed to return. When the nurses got back to the hospital, they found that Catholic nurses and doctors were tending to what was now a facility overflowing with sick and injured Jews. "Christian doctors helped impartially in treating the victims. In most cases they were suffering from head injuries and the results of grotesque attempts at suicide. People had cut their wrists with broken glass and then jumped out of windows or taken some poison or large quantities of sleeping pills. About a hundred people, mostly serious cases, had been brought in. It was still night when the Catholic nurses were compulsorily removed from the hospital, at the orders of the SA."[112]

✡ They're Killing Jews ✡

Inge Berner went to work in Berlin as she did every day. "Across the street was a confectionary. I looked out the window and saw the window of the store was broken and people were taking things from the store and an old couple who owned the store was just sitting inside shaking. I thought, 'What's going on here?' The book keeper came in and said, 'You better go home. They're killing Jews all over Berlin.'"[113]

✡ What Could They Have Eaten? ✡

Gad Beck worked in a clothing store in Berlin. On Kristallnacht all the coats and suits were strewn around the store, but much of the inventory was missing. He started to take some of what they left back to the shelves and discovered that everything he touched was "full of shit." Beck was then sent to look for some boards and ran into a Jew from Berlin who said softly, "You know, the Germans are a strange people. They didn't steal shoes in pairs. They stole single shoes." He gave Beck some boards, and then Beck asked, "Did they do the same thing with you? They shit all over our things." The Berliner answered, "In every shoe," and then he said something Beck said he would never forget: "Man, what could the SA have eaten that would make them shit like that?"[114]

✡ Misplaced Faith ✡

Israel's was a large, independent department store in downtown Berlin. On November 9 one of the employees, who had recently been given an administrative position by the Nazis, warned Wilfrid Israel to keep the store closed the next day. Israel was well connected and thought his store would be safe, so he ignored the warning. Israel seemed to have made the right decision when he opened the store the following morning and a group of police officers suddenly appeared to guard the building. Israel left at one point, and while he was gone, the police left. The SS and others arrived later and proceeded to destroy the store. A fire broke out, but the fire department extinguished it.[115]

✡ Through the Gauntlet ✡

In the village of Kehl, which lies just across a bridge from Strasbourg, Jews were marched through the streets where they were hit, insulted, and spat upon by the townspeople. As they marched through this hostile gauntlet, they were forced to sing, "We have betrayed the German Fatherland. We are responsible for the Paris assassination."[116]

✡ A Sermon for the Nazis ✡

SA men forced their way into the Düsseldorf home of Rabbi Max Eschelbacher shouting, "Vengeance for Paris! Down with the Jews." Eschelbacher recalled, "They pulled wooden hammers out of the bags they were carrying. The next second you could hear the crack of smashed furniture, the crash of broken glass from the cabinets and windows. These ruffians lunged at me with closed fists, one grabbed hold of me and shouted, saying that I should come downstairs. I was certain they were going to kill me." Eschelbacher said good-bye to his wife and left the apartment and found the street filled with 50 to 60 brownshirts. "I was received with the shout: 'Okay, now give us a sermon!' I started to speak about the death of vom Rath, that his murder was a greater misfortune for us than for the German people and that we were innocent when it came to his murder." The rabbi was subsequently taken to jail and remained there for the next 12 days.[117]

✡ No Time to Dress ✡

Henry Eisner was 18 years old. He was sleeping soundly when he was awakened by banging on the door of his house. "We heard some angry voices that asked us to open the doors. For reasons I still don't quite understand, we knew there was major trouble brewing. We didn't open the doors. We went upstairs to the apartment, the second storey of the house, to the apartment of my grandmother. We thought it would be difficult for the people coming after us to get to the second floor, but I remember after we refused to open the doors, they brought tall ladders on which they climbed to reach the second floor. They broke the windows and came into my grandmother's apartment and said they wanted us all to come with them because we were all under arrest. The synagogue was on fire and the retail stores had been broken and their showcases and windows had been broken. They simply told us, 'Don't even get dressed,' or gave us hardly time to get dressed. I know I didn't even have shoes. They took us to a collection point not far from where we lived where all the Jews in the town were rounded up.

"My brother was not home. My mother, father, grandmother and I were all taken to the collection point. My brother was in Berlin and escaped being arrested by hiding in garbage cans. It was 2–3 a.m. when this happened. The women were told they could leave after awhile; my father and I were subsequently loaded on buses and they took us to Buchenwald."[118]

✡ Dying in My Arms ✡

Robert Meier lived in a hotel in Ludwigshafen and got a warning on November 9 from someone he knew in the SS who told him something was going to happen that night. "I stayed away from the hotel until midnight. I figured nothing happened. Everything should be in good shape. But they did not come in until about two, three o'clock in the morning, broke the windows in the hotel, got in, broke all the dishes on the first floor, and they left. Two hours later, the Gestapo returned and picked up everybody in the hotel from all five floors.

"I was living all the way on the top floor. We had to go down the steps from the fifth floor all the way down to the first floor, and on each step was somebody waiting with a stick. They would beat us up from the fifth floor all the way down to the first floor. I had never gone down steps as fast as I went down there."

Meier and the other hotel residents were taken to the local police station. The cells had room for two or three people and they jammed 20 to 25 people into the room. Later, more Jews were brought in and the prison was filled up. Meier recognized a man from his building. "He was beaten up and both his ribs were broken, and he could hardly breathe. I was holding the gentleman for a little while and, finally, I see that he had a heart attack and he died right in my arms. I asked the guards to remove the gentleman. They would not remove him until about an hour later. I felt very bad about it because I happened to know the gentleman, and that's something I never forgot because I was 17-years-old at the time, and I just could never forget it."

About 5 o'clock in the afternoon, several hundred Jews were loaded into police wagons and taken to Durlach castle, which was about six miles from Karlsruhe. Meier described what happened next: "They lined us up. There was a fellow sitting on top there, Gestapo, and he said, 'To the right, to the left.' We didn't know if you went to the right, you were eventually released. To the left, you went to Dachau concentration camp. This showed you how the fellow did it. A friend of mine who was the same age as me, in front of me, he was sent to Dachau, I was not sent to Dachau. I did not know what's going to happen."

The remaining prisoners were taken to the second floor of the castle where they found more Jews, elderly people over 65 and younger people under the age of 16. "All of a sudden the fellow comes in with six fellows with rifles. They were loading the rifles, and I said, 'That's what they are going to do, they are going to get rid of us, and that's the end of that story. But they didn't. All they wanted to do was scare us. So what they did was load the rifle and the guy said, 'Get out.'

"Afterward, we got out of the castle and a crowd of four, five hundred people were waiting outside for us. I walked past everybody. I went right back to the hotel, which was maybe an hour, hour and a half walk. I could not enter the hotel. A fellow was standing there, a guard, who said not to go back into the hotel, it's closed.

"What was I going to do? It was midnight. At 11 o'clock I was released from the castle, it took me an hour to walk, so it was 12 o'clock. . . . I knew some people who lived very close by to this hotel. I rang the bell, nobody answered. I rang a second time. Finally, the third time, the lady I happened to know opened the door and she said, 'My husband was picked up today, he was sent to Dachau.' I said, 'Could you do me a favor? I would like to sleep here overnight. I don't care if it's the floor, whatever it is, for a few hours I can rest up.' Well I was able to sleep there 'til five, six in the morning.

"I called up my mother, who was living in Landau. She told me my father had been picked up. This was the 11th of November. I said, 'Well, I'm going to come over.'

"I took a taxi in Karlsruhe for Landau, and I got into Landau, and I went to our house. Naturally, everything was destroyed. The furniture was all ripped apart. Paintings and everything was ripped apart. The lights were out and I said to my mother, 'What are you going to do?' And she says, 'Well, we can't stay here. They told us we have until one o'clock this afternoon to leave.' No more Jews were allowed in this town, and everybody had to leave."[119]

✡ What Shall We Do? ✡

Jacob Wiener was living in a school dormitory in the port city of Bremen in northwestern Germany where he was a student and also taught Spanish. In the middle of the night, about 2:30 or 3:30 a.m., he heard noises. Jacob got up and said to the other students living with him, "'The best thing is we get dressed now. And if anything should happen, we are ready to encounter whatever there is.' And I said, 'Let's get our bags ready, if anything should happen.' And then I said, 'Let's maybe hide under the bed, or in that corner.' And then I decided, 'No, we shouldn't hide. We should just meet it head-on.'"

Jacob tried to lock the door, but it was no use. "They came in, and they saw our suitcases there. And they said, 'Take these suitcases and throw them against the window.' They wouldn't fall outside the window because the windows were barricaded. Then I said to them, 'What shall we do?'

"'Stay here and wait until we give you orders. And you should know, we never even bent a hair of a Jew, and we won't do it this time, but, eventually, you will all be exterminated,' something like that. I don't know if they said the exact words."

After the Germans left, the students went downstairs and found that the intruders had cut the electric lamps, which were now hanging loosely, and they had also ripped out the faucet so water was spraying out. A non-Jewish woman who lived downstairs came and made them coffee and offered the students food around 4 a.m. About two hours later, the Nazis returned.

They were in civilian clothes and told the students to pack a few things. Jacob thought he should pack everything, but the Nazis said they didn't need to worry, that they would be coming back. Around 7:30 a.m., the students were told to start marching. About 50 or 60 people were marching together in a line toward a prison. They passed the synagogue, which was burning. As they walked through the narrow streets, people stood and watched. Some spat and threw stones at them.

When the marchers reached the prison, the Germans processed each Jew. "The Germans were very methodical. When you came in, they took a picture of you, on the right side, from the left side, from the front. And they took all your money, or all kinds of things which you had in your pocket. And they made a complete record of it. They were very meticulous. They were very orderly in that sense. And they gave it to us, and they said, 'Sign here.' Okay, we signed. Then they led us into cells, prison cells. And I was in prison cell number 99, I think. And there were about 15 boys in that prison cell. They put us in there. And there was, like, a toilet, a bowl. And there were windows on top, with iron bars. I don't think there was anything else, maybe a few mattresses or so. And in the door was a little window. And through this window they gave us food about an hour later, like water with a few beans in it and things like that."

Wiener stayed in the prison for the next eight days. "And we always thought we would all be sent away because every morning and every evening they took us all out. Once a day, they led us around the prison yard to give us a prison walk for an hour. And then they led us all out, and they read a list of names to make sure everyone was still there. And every day the number had become less. And we imagined, because no one told us, that they probably were sent to concentration camps. And then came the last day of the seven days. They called a list, and they read all the names. Then they read seven names, and I was among the seven whom they read. And they said to them, 'Stay at the side.' We stayed at the side."[120]

✡ Get Out of Germany ✡

Gary Matzdorff was an apprentice in Berlin. "I started my apprenticeship when I was 14 and a half in 1936. I learned a leather trade, as a craftsman. Once a week, every apprentice had to go to trade school and that was my day. In the morning, on the bus, I already noticed roving bands smashing store windows, some others painting the word 'Jude' on the window, and then the others would smash the windows. So I sort of crawled in the back of the bus and I had to change over to a streetcar to get to the trade school, and there was a fire in a backyard, in a courtyard, of a building. So I stopped and asked some people what was going on. There was no fire department, and someone said, 'Oh some Jew house is burning.' Apparently, it was a small orthodox synagogue. By watching that for a moment, I was tardy in school. I was the only Jewish student in school, and books started flying toward me as I opened the door. So I closed the door again and just walked the corridor for a minute, or just stood there, stunned. When the door opened, the teacher came out and handed me the books, and he said, 'I had to do this for the class.' And he said, 'Get a hold of your father real quick and try to get out of Germany as quickly as possible. Terrible things are going to happen. Good luck.' And that was it.

"I went downstairs to a phone booth, called home, but my father was already on his way to his office, and mother didn't know anything about it. So I waited another half-hour, forty-five minutes, and called my dad in his office. And he saw the same thing, and he says, 'Call me back in about an hour, I'll see if I can make some arrangements,' which I did. In the meantime, my father got a hold of a friend of his, who was not Jewish, and he was a customer as well, and made some arrangements. He said, 'Meet me at a certain subway station, and then we'll discuss where we're going to go.' He said he doesn't want to mention anything over the phone. So we met, and we rode the subway all day long. When we saw somebody that looked like Gestapo, the typical short-cropped haircut look, we got off the train, walked over to the other side, and went in the other direction. Fortunately, we were never caught during that day and, since it was November, it got dark early. Then we finally slipped into his friend's apartment, which was right in the center of the city, and we stayed there for two weeks."[121]

✡ Martyr's Pride ✡

Anna Becker (later Bluethe) lived in Kaiserslautern. The family's connection to this region of Germany near the French border dated from the late 1690s. "Vater [Anna's husband, Leo] had been arrested by the Gestapo and taken to a collection station. He had the indescribable presence of mind before his departing to leave his keys on the desk of his office (located within our apartment). The house safe was open. On the desk was the strongbox containing about 3,700 Reichsmark. Important documents, usually kept in the safe, had been thrown all over the room, which was in total disarray. I retrieved whatever I could, hastily, put it back in the strongbox and returned it to the safe, which I closed and locked. My hands were shaking while I was doing this. Not only was I terribly nervous but I had never before concerned myself with the safe. It was a blessing that I had the keys to lock the safe. Had its contents remained in the open, they would have disappeared with most of the other possessions, during the second search of the apartment, and the further destruction and devastation which resulted from it.

"My next move was to run to the hall closet. There, amongst some rolls of wool, I had previously hidden 1,000 Reichsmark in anticipation of such an emergency, as now existed. However, due to the total disarray caused by the search, I was, at first, unable to find the money. Finding my large handbag, I took the rolls of wool with its contents, as well as some of my jewelry, stuffed all of it into this handbag and held on to it for dear life. I was naïve to think that after the first search we would not be molested any further and, together with Christine, our faithful and reliable maid, we started to clean up some of the mess. Everything stored in the closets and drawers had been thrown on the floor. A carton with toilet articles, the bottles broken and empty, was lying in a corner. A bag with washing powder had busted and the powder covered the better part of the room. It was a monumental task and we made little headway.

"Suddenly a group of Brownshirts stormed into the apartment, tore out the telephone, threw some of the typewriters through the windows into the street, demolished tables, chairs, anything and everything they could lay their hands on and disappeared as suddenly as they had arrived. While this was going on, passersby stopped outside the house; people from the surrounding houses looked out of their windows and, in time, a mob assembled, watching Christine, who had gone outside to salvage what she could, and handing it back to me through the windows, which were on street level. Some of the people told her not to help me but let me do the cleaning up by myself. In time they threatened her, that she would be harmed if she continued with this work. She therefore came inside, and we tried to continue with the task of cleaning up.

"Within a short time we were again interrupted by more stormtroopers who demanded that Grossvater [Anna's father, Simon Becker] and I report to the police. Grandfather was 86-years-old and had remained in a backroom of the apartment during all the earlier gruesome occurrences. He was still in his bathrobe and wore bedroom slippers. I quickly put some clothing on him, grabbed my Persian lamb coat, in order to have also an object of warmth as well as value should we be transported somewhere else. It still amazes me how much presence of mind and logical thinking one can display under such trying conditions.

"Thus we started to walk through crowds, which were gazing and staring at us in their hostile manner, towards the police station. It was slow progress. Grandfather had developed heart palpitation, had trouble breathing and only made it to the station with the greatest effort. The officer at the police station, to whom we reported and gave our personal particulars, was very correct and polite and asked us to return home after completing his task.

"On our way home I overheard one woman saying, 'How high and unintimidated she holds her head.' At that moment she could not have said anything more encouraging and uplifting to me.

"Arrogance was not normally in my character, perhaps some deep hidden martyr pride of our ancestors manifested itself. I wanted to show these people that they could not bring us down.

"Hardly had we returned home when another group of thugs burst into our apartment. A particular big and threatening one of the group, obviously the leader, shouted: 'What are you still doing here and why have you not reported to the police station?' I responded in a very calm manner that we had just returned from there, and had been told by the police to do so. This, however, made no impression on him and he ordered us in an even more vehement manner to do so at once. Thinking that this brute was acting on his own accord, I asked him for his authorization for this demand. At this he really hit the top and in the loudest voice that he could muster, proclaimed: 'I do not need any authorization. I am a national socialist. Report to the police at once.'

"I went into the kitchen, finding grandfather sitting on a box behind the door trying to put on his shoes. As he had difficulties lacing his shoes, I tried to help him. At this, the brute threw something at the overhead light and covered both of us with the splinters from the glass. Fortunately, neither one of us got hurt. I asked the man to let me help my old father to get dressed but he would not hear of it and shouted, 'The old Jew has been around long enough. Get going!' And with this, we again were on our way to the station. Fortunately, the distance was not far. When we arrived there and told the officer our story he asked us to point out the person who had ordered us to return. I turned around to do so, but he had disappeared. And so we again made our way home.

"Yet, our ordeal was far from over. A new group of Nazis stormed into the apartment. These were armed with large crowbars and my impression was they were going to use these to kill us. This was not their intention. Instead, they searched for the office and directed their fury on all the objects not utterly destroyed by the earlier invasions. The furniture in the office consisted of a bookcase with glass doors, a large writing desk with several drawers on either side and also the heavy house safe, which I had previously mentioned.

"The vandalism which they caused defies description. The glass doors of the bookcase were the first object of their wrath. All the books were torn off the shelves and either thrown on the floor or through the windows into the street. A similar fate awaited all the papers, documents and other matters, which father kept in his writing desk. Having this accomplished they overturned all the furniture including the heavy safe (fortunately leaving the door facing upwards) but throwing part of the other furniture on top of the safe. It was an utter devastation which was left after their departure.

"Not trusting that this would be the end of our ordeal, I told grandfather to put on his best suit and most comfortable shoes and I myself got dressed in some warm clothes and also my best fitting shoes. I was convinced that we would be arrested and shipped to some unknown destination. Our getting dressed took much longer than normally. Due to the vandalism of the home we had to search for our clothes, then move into some protected corner of the apartment, as stones were thrown from the street into it, from time to time.

"My earlier fears were justified. We had barely finished getting dressed when yet another group stormed into the house. Again they were carrying heavy crowbars and demanded to be shown the living room. This room had previously been ignored but it now received the full fury and destructive power of the beasts. It took three of them to rip the heavy chandelier out of the ceiling. The glass enclosed display case, containing so many precious glasses, cups, saucers, crystal bowls and many other valuable objects were thrown on the floor and smashed. Systematically, they went from room to room, standing lamps were thrown over, marble slabs smashed, mirrors and any remaining unbroken windows encountered the same fate. In our bedroom, the big tile stove, reaching almost to the ceiling, was toppled over and in the kitchen every egg and all the preserves, stored in glasses, were systematically smashed on the floor. Being satisfied that the destruction had been completed, we were finally left alone.

"As the physical danger to us had abated for the moment, my thoughts and anxiety turned to father and the awareness what these people could do to human beings if they reacted like this to material objects. However, we were not allowed to have thoughts of this type for long, before the next bombardment of stones through our glassless windows started. It was early afternoon by now, the schoolchildren had been dismissed from their classrooms and, following in the steps of their parents and elders, they willingly participated in the Jew-baiting and destruction. The teachings and instructions of the last years bore their fruit. Slowly, the mob outside our house dispersed and the area around us became quiet."

A Jewish neighbor offered to take Anna's father to the basement of her house. "This place, because it was accessible only through a side entrance, had been overlooked and remained undemolished. Several families fleeing from the mob, while their homes were being destroyed, had taken refuge in this basement hideout. I was relieved to know grandfather would be in a somewhat safer place, and I almost welcomed the thought of being alone at home."

Anna was afraid her husband would return home and not know what happened to her and her father, so she went back to her house and found someone stealing some of their belongings. "I took them out of his hands and evidently intimidated him sufficiently for him to leave without a further word. To my great joy and relief, father appeared soon afterwards. All internees over 50 years old had been released. He was aghast over the destruction which had been caused while he was away."

Policemen came later and took her husband away for about an hour. Shortly after he returned, a group of storm troopers burst into their apartment and said all Jews were being expelled and had to be out of the province by midnight of that day. After living in the area for more than 200 years her family was being driven from their home overnight.[122]

CHAPTER 6

Synagogues Aflame

It is difficult to say that the destruction of buildings or books was more catastrophic than the physical attacks on Jews—the arrests and the incarceration of men in concentration camps—but the destruction of synagogues, Torah scrolls, and prayer books was perhaps even more devastating. This attacked the very spirit and the soul of the Jewish people. Even as the treatment of Jews varied from time to time and place to place in Germany, the houses of prayer, existing for decades and in many cases, centuries, were symbols of the long-standing Jewish roots in Germany.

As the birthplace of the Reform movement of Judaism, Germany also represented one of the cradles of Jewish religious intellectualism. For Orthodox Jews, the attacks on the synagogues were devastating blows to their heart. Jews who were not observant, however, were also shocked and hurt by the devastation because they too understood the importance of the symbols to their religion and peoplehood.

The Nazis understood this and specifically targeted synagogues for vengeance. A few synagogues were destroyed even before Kristallnacht, such as the one in Munich that apparently had drawn the ire of Hitler. Benno Cohn of the Berlin Zionist Organization reported that he was told that Hitler had seen the synagogue on a trip to the city and asked what it was. After being told it was a synagogue, he reportedly declared, "When I come to Munich next time, I don't want to see this building again!" The synagogue and the adjoining Jewish community building were destroyed in June 1938. In August the main synagogue in Nuremberg was also demolished because it was "spoiling the look of the city."[123]

Orders to destroy synagogues throughout Germany and Austria went out on November 9–10. For example, the following order was given by a group commander on November 10: "All Jewish synagogues in the area of Brigade 50 have to be blown up or set afire. . . . The operation will be carried out in civilian clothing. . . . Execution of the order will be reported."[124]

Synagogues were attacked in small towns all over Germany and Austria. In Zeven in Lower Saxony, for example, only 28 Jews lived among the 2,500 residents. Everything was removed from inside the synagogue and burned in the town square. By 1938 only a handful of Jews still lived in Weisweiler, and the synagogue, little more than a prayer room, had not been used in three years. Still, it became a target of destruction, along with the few remaining Jewish houses and stores.[125] The Austrian town of Eisenstadt didn't have any Jews left after the German annexation, but the synagogue they left behind was still destroyed. In the town of Emmerich, Jews were forced to set fire to their synagogue.[126]

Large towns and cities, many of which had large, well-established Jewish communities, suffered the same fate. Dozens of synagogues were pillaged and burned in Berlin and Vienna. The oldest Jewish area in Germany was in Regensburg. Jews had been living there for more than 900 years. The synagogue dated to 1841. It was destroyed on Kristallnacht, and the Jewish men were forced to march through the streets holding a banner that said, "The removal of the Jews." They were ultimately sent to Dachau.[127]

German newspapers unapologetically reported on the destruction of synagogues, taking their cue from the propaganda ministry to suggest this was a natural consequence following the assassination of vom Rath in Paris. The *Fränkischer Kurier*, for example, noted the anger of the people intensifying through the night. "The synagogues on Essenweinstraße in Nuremberg and in Fürth were set on fire during the night of Wednesday to Thursday. Both synagogues were completely gutted by fire. The fire department, which was on the scene immediately, prevented the flames from spreading. The Jewish stores and businesses were demolished, windows smashed, and the inventory of shops were tossed about. There was no looting anywhere. The goods are still lying strewn about in the Jewish shops."[128]

Similarly, the editor of *Hohenzollerische Blatter* described the destruction of the synagogue in Hechingen, which had been used since 1775: "During the night of Wednesday to Thursday, indignant *Volksgenossen* gathered on Goldschmiedestraße in front of the synagogue. In completely understandable and justifiable anger, they had seized on this Jewish place of worship to vent their will for vengeance. Within a short period of time, the doors had been broken in and the entire interior furnishings and fixtures had been destroyed. In their inordinate anger, the *Volksgenossen* went about their work so thoroughly that it will be impossible to restore the interior furnishings to their previous purpose."[129]

Some synagogues were spared. In most cases, this was not because the Germans in those locations felt any reluctance about destroying a house of prayer; these synagogues were protected out of self-interest.

Some synagogues were built into a block of residences or were very close to the homes or businesses of non-Jews, and the arsonists, as well as the firefighters, were afraid they might accidentally burn Aryan property. A number of witnesses testified that some Germans stood up to the mobs that did not consider the danger to the non-Jewish area and made sure they did not set fires. Of course, in most of those instances, the rabble was allowed to go inside the synagogues and to commit as much mayhem as possible. Frequently, the Torah scrolls and prayer books were thrown into the street, where they could be burned without endangering the neighborhoods. In many of the other cases where the synagogues were torched, witnesses reported seeing firefighters or police officers simply standing by and watching the destruction.

Some of the most vivid descriptions come from Berliners who witnessed the destruction of the largest synagogue in Berlin, the Fasanenstrasse Synagogue, as well as other temples in the capital. To get a sense of how Berlin's Jewish population was integrated into the city and how this synagogue had once been viewed by the population, consider the following excerpts from the *Berliner Tageblatt* of August 26, 1912, describing the synagogue's dedication:

> *The festive dedication of the new synagogue on Fasan-enstrasse took place at midday today in the presence of the highest representatives of government, the military, and the city. . . . At 12 o'clock sharp the personal representative of the Kaiser, his military adjutant Colonel General Excellency von Kessel arrived. He was seated on a seat of honor on the bimah. Next to him sat the Under-secretary in the Ministry of the Interior Holtz.*

> *In the first row one could see the representative of the Ministry of Religious Affairs, Director von Chappius . . . and for the High Command of the Armed Forces Colonel von Brauchitsch. The city of Berlin was represented by Lord Mayor Wermuth, . . . The Chief of Police von Jagow in the uniform of a cavalry colonel, and his deputy, Councilor Friedheim. In addition many representatives of the Protestant and Catholic clergy were present as well as all of the rabbis of the Berlin Jewish community. . . . The ceremony started with a festive procession of the Torah scrolls through the synagogue accompanied by songs by a choir and organ music after which the scrolls were placed into the arc. After a singing by the congregation led by the cantor, Rabbi Bergmann carried out the beautiful ceremony at the lighting of the eternal light. In his address he said that just as the light of this lamp so the love of fatherland of this community will never extinguish.*

On November 10, 1938, 26 years, 2 months, and 15 days after this dedication ceremony, the synagogue was destroyed.[130]

✡ Running into the Fire ✡

Firefighters stood and watched the Fasanenstrasse Synagogue burn. The reader of the synagogue, a man named Davidsohn, pleaded with the captain of the firefighters to put out the fire. "Turn on the hoses," he cried to the fire chief, who stood dumbly watching the spectacle with his men. "Get out of here. You'll get yourself killed," the captain snarled. "I'm afraid I can't help. We've come to protect the neighboring buildings."

"For the love of God, let me at least bring out the sacred objects."

"Just then there was a sound of pounding, and Wolfsohn, the porter, staggered into the courtyard in bloodstained nightclothes. He had refused to surrender the keys to the sanctuary and the doors had been forced. The 78-stop organ was heaved over a balcony. The bronze candelabra was taken down and the scrolls of the Law and their appointments torn and broken. Rabbinical garments were cut to shreds and prayer books were mutilated. Then the SA and SS commandos drenched the wooden benches in petrol, and fire leapt through the building. Davidsohn vainly tried to enter. At five o'clock, when the fire had subsided to smoldering ashes, the mob began to disperse, the firemen rode off and the man who for twenty-seven years had led the community's prayers bowed to recite the Kaddish, the prayer for the dead, before the smoking rubble."[131]

One of the witnesses was Selma Schiratzki. As she left her Berlin home on the morning of November 10, she saw a woman who seemed upset. When Selma asked her what was wrong, the woman answered with tears running down her face, 'Something so horrible has happened, I can hardly tell you. Just think—all the synagogues are burning.'"

Selma lived in the western part of Berlin and used to take the train to school. "When the train passed the synagogue in Fasanenstrasse, I saw with horror the smoke rising from the ruins. Then I heard a man next to me say to his son: 'There you can see what has happened! And remember, if I should ever find out that you have had a part in things like these, you would no longer be a son of mine.'"[132]

Ernest Günter Fontheim had celebrated his bar mitzvah in the synagogue in Fasanenstrasse. He was still a teenager when it burned. When he went to school, he didn't notice anything unusual. "When I entered my classroom, some of my classmates were telling horror stories of what they had seen on their way to school, like smashed store windows of Jewish-owned shops, looting mobs, and even burning synagogues. A fair number of students were absent.

"The 8 o'clock bell rang signaling the beginning of classes, but no teachers were in sight either in our class or in any of the other classes along our corridor. That had never happened before. I don't remember anymore how long it took for the teachers to emerge from the teacher's conference room. It finally opened and the teachers streamed out to their various class rooms; they all looked extremely grim.

"When our teacher, Dr. Wollheim, entered the room and closed the door, all talking stopped instantly, and there was complete silence in the class. That too was unique, for, in general, we were a fairly undisciplined bunch, and it usually took several admonitions until some quiet was established. In a tense voice Dr. Wollheim announced that school was being dismissed because our safety could not be guaranteed. This was followed by a number of instructions which he urged us to follow in every detail. Number one, we should go home directly and as fast as possible without lingering anywhere or visiting friends so that our parents would know that we are safe. Number two, we should not walk in large groups because that would attract attention and possible violence by hostile crowds. He concluded by saying that there would be no school for the foreseeable future and that we would be notified when school would reopen again.

"I quickly walked back to the Tiergarten Station and decided to look out the window when the elevated train would pass the Synagogue Fasanenstrasse where I had become bar mitzvah. It was a beautiful structure built in Moorish style with three large cupolas. I literally felt my heart fall into my stomach when I saw a thick column of smoke rising out of the center cupola. There was no wind, and the column seemed to stand motionless reaching into the heavens. At that moment all rationality left me. I got off the train at the next stop and raced back the few blocks as if pulled by an irresistible force. I did not think of Dr. Wollheim's instruction nor of any possible danger to myself. Police barricades kept a crowd of onlookers on the opposite sidewalk. Firefighters were hosing down adjacent buildings. The air was filled with the acrid smell of smoke. I was wedged in the middle of a hostile crowd, which was in an ugly mood shouting anti-Semitic slogans. I was completely hypnotized by the burning synagogue and was totally oblivious to any possible danger. I thought of the many times I had attended services there and listened to the sermons all of which had fortified my soul during the difficult years of persecution. Even almost six years of Nazi rule had not prepared me for such an experience.

"Suddenly, someone shouted that a Jewish family was living on the ground floor of the apartment building across the street from the synagogue. Watching the fire, the crowd was backed against the building. Someone else shouted: 'Let's get them!' Everyone turned around. Those closest surged through the building entrance. I could hear heavy blows against the apartment door.

"In my imagination I pictured a frightened family hiding in a room as far as possible from the entrance door—hoping and praying that the door would withstand—and I prayed with them. I vividly remember the crashing violent noise of splintering wood followed by deadly silence, then suddenly wild cries of triumph. An elderly bald-headed man was brutally pushed through the crowd while fists rained down on him from all sides accompanied by anti-Semitic epithets. His face was bloodied. One single man in the crowd shouted: 'How cowardly! So many against one!'

"He was immediately attacked by others. After the elderly Jew had been pushed to the curb, a police car appeared mysteriously; he was put in and driven off. I left this scene of horror completely drained, incredulous, in a trance and went home. . . . What has remained and will forever remain in my memory is the image of the thick column of smoke standing on top of the center cupola of that beautiful synagogue and the bloodied bald head of an unknown Jew."[133]

George Ginsburg saw a red sky as 20 synagogues burned in Berlin. He saw Brownshirts running through the streets arresting and beating Jews, and trucks taking people away to Sachsenhausen. "I was in bed and woke up when I got a telephone call from Betar [a Zionist youth group]. I was told to get outside immediately and I'd be picked up by a Betar truck because we had to run in the shuls to save the Torah. We did run in the burning shuls. I didn't have any fear then. I was young. We ran in and saved whatever we could. . . . I ran inside Fasanen-strasse synagogue. It was smoking and black. There were four or five of us. We made a chain to pass on things. The older ones ran right inside and we were standing halfway and I saved a few *Torot* [Torah scrolls].

They would take them and hide them in the Betar headquarters. Outside, there were people standing with bars who started hitting us. Some people were bleeding and we ran away. We ran to private houses where our members lived and then I came home."[134]

Eva Bergmann was in bed in her Berlin home around midnight when Kristallnacht began for her. "We heard all of a sudden loud clattering in the street and we heard that it was glass shattering. Voices were screaming. We didn't dare to look out the window. We were afraid. Only the next morning we looked down and saw on the street—there were a lot of Jewish groceries and tailors and carpenters—and there was a lot of glass on the street and people were trying to sweep the glass away. We were horrified. Around 5 p.m. we went out and saw the nearby synagogue. Glass was all taken out. In the yard were torn up prayer books and ashes all over. The synagogue was hardly recognizable. Even though we never went to the synagogue it was a horrible experience for the Jewish people. We saw some people cleaning up the ashes in the courtyard."[135]

Inge Berner heard that synagogues were burning in Berlin. "The synagogue that we went to was too far away for us to see it. That one was saved because there was a police officer who would not let the mob burn it down. It was in the middle of a residential neighborhood and he said if you burn it down then all the houses around it will burn down and he didn't let them. That synagogue was saved." It was later bombed in an air raid.[136]

Eva Brewster saw the synagogue in Berlin the day after it had been set ablaze. "It was just ruins. It's impossible to describe my feelings. It was about the same as burning all the books. Everything that was German culture, everything that I was brought up with. I think the whole culture was brought down to a lowest common denominator and that was a very low one."[137]

Norbert Wollheim was going outside the morning of November 10 when someone told him the synagogues were burning throughout Berlin. "I couldn't believe it. I went to the synagogue where I was bar mitzvahed, and where I'd been married, and I saw the flames coming from the roof, from the cupola of this beautiful edifice. The fire engines were standing by doing nothing, only protecting the buildings next to it. I still couldn't believe it. I thought, maybe it's the only one, so I went to another major synagogue in West Berlin, and it, too, was burning and already partly in ruins.

"I thought, this is the people you were brought up with, these are the poets and the thinkers. What happened to German civilization? The people standing with me in front of the burning synagogues didn't dare to say a word. They may have felt ashamed, but they didn't dare to say so, because this was one of the principles the Nazis had established: they had concentration camps for anybody who said anything against them.

"There were also quite a number who made very nasty remarks. There was glee among them. They said, 'The Jews got what they deserve,' and so on. That really gave me the shock of my life. I saw it, but I couldn't digest it, not intellectually and not emotionally.

"Then my wife came to me and said, 'Norbert, you're not going home.' I asked why. She said that the police were going around taking men into custody and she'd arranged for me to stay with the mother of a friend who had just left for America. She was alone and would feel more protected if I stayed with her. Arrangements had also been made for my father to take shelter in the apartment of a sister who was a widow. That's what he did, unaware of what the next step would be.

"I spent a couple of nights away from my apartment—I was still free to roam around—and I saw what had happened in the main streets of Berlin, the Jewish stores that had been smashed and vandalized and looted. Then I realized that Rabbi Leo Baeck, who was my teacher and spiritual mentor, was right when he said that the historical hour of German Jewry had come to an end."[138]

✡ A Grisly Picture ✡

Grynszpan had studied in the yeshiva in Frankfurt am Main, so it was not surprising that the city would be a particular target of Nazi wrath. Of 43 synagogues in Frankfurt am Main, at least 21 were destroyed. Hitler Youth members began their rampage in that city at 5:00 a.m. on November 10. At 6:30 a.m., the Gestapo began to arrest Jewish men. A German exiles group, Sopade, reported on the violence that ensued: "All of the synagogues are completely destroyed. They offer a grisly picture of devastation. . . . The big synagogue on Friedberger Anlage, a beautiful and quite recent construction, burned to the ground. Firefighters looked on without making an attempt to extinguish the fire. The large West End synagogue, just like the other old synagogues, became a prey of the flames. Windows in all Jewish stores were broken, and everything inside, large and small, smashed. It looked tragic at Ehrenfeld's, a gift store on the Zeil. Expensive radios and photographic devices

lay destroyed in the demolished shop window. . . . Windows and
shutters at Voltz-Eberle, a wine store chain, were [also] destroyed
and wine was poured into the alley. . . . Shops previously owned
by Jews and now under Gentile management affixed signs reading
'Now Aryan Property.' At Reta, a sundries store, it was written that
ownership of the business was falling into Gentile hands. In front
of many stores also stood police detachments. They appeared, however, only after the destruction had finished. It [the pogrom] looks
like a premeditated undertaking."[139]

✡ A White Snake ✡

Batya Emanuel was 13 years old when she was awakened by her
mother and watched as her father called the police to report that
the synagogue behind their house was being vandalized. Batya
rushed to the bedroom window so she could see what was going
on in the synagogue. "Through its windows we saw the chandelier swing like a pendulum, moved by invisible hands, swaying
backward and forward in ever-widening revolutions—crash—
darkness. A window was pushed open, a chair flew out, tumbled
to the ground and broke into splinters. It was followed by another
chair and yet another, and then there was silence. What were they
up to now? We had not long to wait: a white snake jumped down
from the windowsill and slithered down, down to the ground below,
it seemed unending.

'Scrolls of the Law, Torah scrolls,' we gasped, not wanting to
believe our eyes. Papa ran back to our room, which overlooked

the street. He returned a moment later: 'Yes, they're there, several policemen on the other side of the street—waiting for those godless vandals to complete their work of destruction.'"[140]

✡ Your Jew Temple Is Burning ✡

In Breslau, a town along the Oder river that is now part of Poland (renamed Wroclaw), Gerda Bikales was alone with a friend. Her father had already gone to America, and the children's mothers were out on an errand. "Suddenly, we heard some commotion in the courtyard. The little Polish shul my father went to was in that courtyard. We heard glass shattering and lots of people laughing. We looked out and saw a fire. They had set the building on fire. We opened the window and asked, 'What's going on here?' We're 7- and 8-years-old, alone. Someone said, 'Your Jew temple is burning,' and laughed. They took out the Torahs and threw them around in the courtyard. Soon thereafter our mothers hurried in and we huddled together not knowing what to do. They did stop the fire because there were apartments all around, so the fire was not a danger to us except initially when we didn't understand what was happening.... I imagine the people who burned the synagogue must have lived there because it was a little shtiebel and you had to know it was there. I don't think we had a radio so we had no sense how widespread this was, if this was an aberration, just in Breslau. It took us awhile to understand it was a coordinated effort. We were scared."[141]

✡ Floating down the Danube ✡

Siegfried Buchwalter's father had a bayonet from World War I, and his mother went out during the violence in Vienna to hide it because she was afraid of what might happen if the Nazis discovered a weapon in their house. "She came back and told us stories that Jews were being dragged out of their houses, the burning of the synagogues. It was amazing how well the attacks were organized. The synagogues were nestled between apartment houses so if you didn't have an expert dynamiting it you could have damaged the adjoining apartment house. It was done by experts because only the synagogues were damaged. The Torah scrolls were floating down the Danube and burning but nothing was happening to the adjoining apartments. It was over by the evening."[142] At least 95 synagogues in Vienna were destroyed.[143]

✡ Nothing but Bare Walls ✡

When Arnold Fleischmann returned to his home in Bayreuth in northern Bavaria, he found the synagogue, which was dedicated in 1760, vandalized.[144] "They were afraid to burn it because it was wall-to-wall with the Bayreuth opera house. It was a very old and beautiful synagogue. There was very little left except the bare walls. They had burned things in the middle of the floor to be sure the walls didn't burn. And it was very close to where my family lived. It was only about four blocks from my family home so this area was right next to the cultural, downtown area of Bayreuth. Today, Bayreuth is an important cultural center and they are rebuilding the synagogue and the attitude is to have Jews return. I returned with my son and we were guests of the mayor. They're trying to make up for what happened, I guess."[145]

✡ The Shock Was in My Legs ✡

It was just a couple of weeks before her 12th birthday when Erna Florsheim was sent home from school. When she got back to Koenigsbach, she saw the synagogue burning. "As we walked down the hill, we saw the Torahs on the ground. We went home and my mother was at the window looking out for us. She knew what was going on. We came to the house and my mother didn't know what to do or where to take us for safety because they destroyed the few Jewish families' homes completely in Koenigsbach. One woman who lived very near to the synagogue grabbed a piece of the Torah and took it in. My mother told me to go get the keys for the apartment of a non-Jewish family living on the first floor. She said maybe we can stay in that apartment.... But I couldn't walk. The shock from it all was in my legs. I returned and told my mother, 'I can't go, I can't walk.' So my mother took us into the garden. It was cool already, it was November. We stayed there until it was night."[146]

✡ Risking Life ✡

Herta Mansbacher was the assistant principal of the Jewish school in the southwestern German town of Worms. When the synagogue in town was set alight, she risked her life by putting out the fire and standing in front of the building to prevent anyone from restarting it. Eventually the mob overwhelmed her, and the synagogue was burned down.[147]

✡ An Unforgettable Smell ✡

Sol Messinger was only six years old on Kristallnacht. "The school that I was at was right next to a synagogue. As a matter of fact, there was sort of a courtyard. The synagogue was in the back of the courtyard. The school was on one side and, in front of this courtyard, separating the courtyard from the street, was the school gym. Well, when my mother took me back to school after Kristallnacht, we came to the school and I saw that all of the windows of the gym were broken. Apparently, that's how they had gotten into the courtyard to get to the synagogue. Then when we walked into the courtyard I could see that the synagogue had been burned down. I could not only see it, I could smell it. You could still smell the smoldering smoke, and I can, it sounds funny, but I can still sort of smell that smell. It's something that you just can't forget. I don't know if you can imagine even what it felt like to know that the synagogue that you had been attending with your parents, I told you I used to go with my father on Saturday mornings, was burned down. It was burned down because people didn't like Jews, namely me. I mean, it was just a terrible, terrible feeling. You really felt violated."[148]

✡ There Must Be Revenge ✡

Alfred Kleeman had returned from Munich to his home in Gaukonigshoken when his school was closed. "I proceeded to go up the street to our synagogue. Well, it wasn't burned to the ground. It wasn't burned at all simply because our local Christian neighbor had a farm right next door, and he persuaded the hoodlums not to burn the synagogue because he was afraid his own properties could go down with the fire. So what did they do then? They took axes, all kinds of hammers, and literally smashed the inside of the synagogue." Alfred saw the benches, books, and Torah scrolls outside burning. Everything left inside was torn to shreds. He described the scene as "a sight that I will never forget" because "our synagogue meant a great deal to me, and to all of us." He told himself, "There must be revenge somewhere for this indescribable act of destruction."

It turned out that everything from the synagogue was not destroyed. The day before, Kleeman's sister had been in a sewing factory in a nearby town and had seen Jewish properties being ruined. She came home early and told her father what was happening. "My father had the foresight, and he sneaked into the synagogue before all of these events took place, and he removed one Torah scroll. I am not sure if this was the Torah scroll that was once donated by someone in our family to the synagogue or whether he just picked one at random. Anyway, he took this Torah scroll and took it into our house and hid it in that very same chamber where they were hiding, in a corner. So, when they took my father out of there, and took him with them, that left my mother and my sister alone. But the Torah scroll they did not see, or perhaps they weren't interested at that time, I don't know. But it was very dark in there and they probably didn't see it."[149]

✡ Let's Throw Her in the Flames ✡

Ursula Rosenfeld was 13 years old, living in Quackenbrack. "The school where I went to was right opposite the synagogue. It was on the same street, in fact. They were two buildings opposite each other. And strangely enough, that morning, when I went to school I saw two SA men, that's Nazi men, in uniform, standing outside our house. I mean, people were in uniform a lot of the time, but it seemed very odd. I don't know. I had a feeling. So there was something strange. We had no wireless. As a child, our information was mainly through the newspaper and, of course, information doesn't travel as quickly. So we didn't know what had happened. And, my father had already gone to work; he was in a nearby small village. He was supervising the loading of timber at a railway station.

"I went to school the usual way, and was sitting in the classroom. I remember it was a French lesson and, suddenly, we could hear very strange noises and then you saw flames shooting up and smelled burning. And all the children dashed out of the classroom onto the street. And there were masses of people lining the streets. And I saw the synagogue was on fire. Now, I don't know what happened to the family that lived downstairs, I think they had already been taken into custody. But it was terrifying. They had thrown all their belongings out into the street, broken things. A little child's pram was bashed to pieces, a doll, and then suddenly two people in uniform came out with the Torah. They were dancing in the street, it sort of had little bells on it, and they thought it was very funny. They were shaking these bells. And people were laughing and shouting and then they saw me and then they said, 'There's another Jew! Let's throw her into the flames too!' And it was a moment in my life I shall never forget.

"You couldn't imagine the atmosphere and the burning. I don't know, the sort of, hysteria of people. I mean, there were people who probably had gone, lived their lives in a perfectly peaceable way. How people can be driven to that kind of hysteria, you can't really imagine. I don't even to this day remember how I got home. I do remember seeing a truck with men, whom they obviously had arrested, from all the nearby villages where Jews lived. And, well, it was difficult to connect, it was only later I learned that they had driven them all into the marketplace. They had arrested my father too. Well, eventually, I got back home, and my mother and grandmother were absolutely distraught. The atmosphere was that we just didn't know what was happening. And that was the end of my school days, really. It was also the end of my family life. I didn't realize that was the end of everything really, as far as my childhood."[150]

✡ A Hitler Youth ✡

Peter Becker was not Jewish. In 1938, he was a nine-year-old Nazi in training attending a Hitler Youth school in Potsdam. Shortly after Kristallnacht he remembered marching in formation with his classmates when they passed a burned building. "Not only was it burned, but the windows had been smashed. By this time we were no longer in formation and sort of walking along. We decided that broken windows lent themselves beautifully to being broken a little bit more. So we picked up stones and threw them into the windows.

The teacher who was supervising us said, 'Don't do this. This is a synagogue and it's in bad shape, but we do not throw stones at it.' We said, 'What is a synagogue?' Of course, it was a Jewish church and that was it. And then we marched on and that was the total extent of my acquaintance with what had happened on the 9th of November."[151]

✡ From Synagogue to Park ✡

At 7 a.m. a policeman appeared at the home of Artur Flehinger, a former teacher in the gymnasiums of Baden-Baden. He was one of 80 Jewish men arrested that morning and taken to the police station. "The SS ordered them to go outside to the courtyard and line up in rows. Towards noon, accompanied by the SS and police, the Jews were marched in long lines through the streets of the city towards the local synagogue. Hundreds of residents of Baden-Baden lined the streets and hurled anti-Semitic epithets at the Jewish prisoners. On the steps of the synagogue, many more Germans awaited to join in the verbal abuse. The Jews were forced to enter the synagogue, to remove their hats and to listen to anti-Semitic lectures from the SS. Afterwards, Artur Flehinger was told to come up to the podium and to read sections from *Mein Kampf*. The SS were not satisfied with his recitation and beat him. A similar fate awaited all those called up to the podium to read. The Jews were then forced to sing the Nazi anthem, 'Horst Wessel,' over and over again until the Nazis were satisfied. After abusing them for many long hours, the Jews (except for the old and feeble) were loaded onto trucks and taken to Dachau. As soon as they were deported, the mob set fire to the synagogue. They tried to throw the synagogue's cantor into the flames, but he was saved by a fireman. The stores and homes of the Jews in Baden-Baden were pillaged; the stone remains of the synagogue were used to pave a road, and a city park was erected where the synagogue once stood."[152]

✡ When Will It Be Our Turn? ✡

A retired fireman recalled Kristallnacht in Laupheim. "The alarm went off between 5–5:30 a.m. and, as usual, I jumped on my bicycle towards the firehouse. I had a strange feeling when I got there and saw many people standing in front of it. I was not allowed to go into the firehouse to take the engines out, or even to open the doors. One of my friends, who lived next to the synagogue, whispered to me, 'Be quiet—the synagogue is burning; I was beaten up already when I wanted to put out the fire.'

"Eventually we were allowed to take the fire engines out, but only very slowly. We were ordered not to use any water till the whole synagogue was burned down. Many of us did not like to do that, but we had to be careful not to voice our opinions, because 'the enemy is listening.'

"Only after one of the party members was worried that his house was going to catch fire, were we allowed to use water. But, even then, we just had to stand and watch until the House of Prayers was reduced to rubble and ashes.

"In the meantime, the marshals rounded up the Jews and dragged them in front of the synagogue, where they had to kneel down and put their hands above their heads. I saw with my own eyes how one old Jew was dragged down and pushed to his knees. Then the arsonists came in their brown uniforms to admire the results of their destruction. . . . Everyone seemed rather quiet and subdued. . . . We had to stand watch at the synagogue to make sure there were no more smoldering sparks. My turn was from 10–11 and 2–3 p.m. The brown uniforms paraded around to admire their work.

"As I was watching the destroyed synagogue and the frail old Jews, I wondered whose turn would be next! . . . When would it be our turn? Will the same thing happen to our Protestant and Catholic Churches."[153]

✡ Firemen Stand By ✡

Henry Stern was 14 years old living in Stuttgart on the morning of November 10: "I was on my way to school when I saw the flames and the smoke rising from the big synagogue (which was adjacent to the Jewish school). The fire engine stood by but did nothing. There was a huge crowd of people standing there and I remember clearly that there was complete silence. (Not a jubilating crowd, as was generally reported in the German press.) I, of course, was in shock and ran home crying."[154]

✡ Burn the Jews! ✡

Ernest Michel recalled watching the synagogue in Mannheim burn. "The brownshirts of the SA had taken out the prayer books, the prayer shawls, the Torah scrolls, everything they could get their hands on. They'd dumped them in a pile on the street and, laughing boisterously, were trampling on them, enjoying themselves. . . . 'Burn the Jews!' they kept chanting. 'Burn the Jews!'"[155]

✡ Gutted by Flames ✡

The American consul in Leipzig, David Buffum, witnessed the destruction of the synagogues in that city. "Three synagogues of Leipzig were fired simultaneously by incendiary bombs and all sacred objects and records desecrated or destroyed, in most instances hurled through the windows and burned in the streets. No attempts were made to quench the fires, functions of the fire brigade having been confined to playing water on adjoining buildings. All of the synagogues were irreparably gutted by flames."[156]

✡ Down with the Jews ✡

Michael Lucas lived in Hoengen, a village near Aachen on the Belgian border, where the small Jewish community had built a synagogue on the meadow he owned opposite his home. A mob approached the synagogue shouting, "Down with the Jews." Michael watched with horror as the crowd smashed the Holy Ark and tossed the Torah scrolls as if they were balls before heaving them out the door into the muddy street. Children stomped on the parchment while others tore them to pieces and stole the silver adornments that had covered them.

According to his nephew, Lucas tried to run outside, but his wife held him back fearing the rabble would kill him. "He leaned against the wall, tears streaming from his eyes, like those of a little child." Soon he heard the sound of hammers and saw that men were on the roof cutting the cross beams and throwing down the tiles. It did not take long to reduce the building to rubble. "Where the two well-cared-for flower beds had flanked both sides of the gravel path leading to the door of the synagogue, the children had lit a bonfire and the parchment of the scrolls gave enough food for the flames to eat up the smashed up benches and doors, and the wood which only the day before had been the Holy Ark for the Scrolls of the Law of Moses."[157]

✡ Enough Now ✡

Jewish men from the towns of Altdorf and Schmieheim were marched through the street in nearby Kippenheim taunted by Hitler Youth who threw rocks and dung at them as they passed. Then the young Nazis set the synagogue on fire and threw all the books, Torah scrolls, and whatever else they could find into the brook running through the town. Ilse Wertheimer hid as the hooligans began to break the windows and vandalize the homes and businesses of the Jews. "We women watched behind the curtains in the living room, wondering how soon they would break the door down and kill us. They tried to break our front door when Dr. Bernhard Weber in his SS uniform yelled, 'That's enough now, stop!' I think that saved our lives."[158]

✡ Rescuing a Star ✡

The Semper synagogue in Dresden was designed by Gottfried Semper, the same man who created the city's opera house. It went up in flames on Kristallnacht, but a German firefighter, Alfred Neugebauer, rescued a golden Star of David that had been on top of the synagogue. He hid it in a box of sand for more than 60 years. When a new synagogue was consecrated on the same site in 2001, Neugebauer was given the honor of attaching it above the entrance.[159]

✡ Blazing Dome ✡

Hans Berger was living in Wiesbaden. "When on the morning of the 10th of November I was driving my car to work, as I did every day, my route took me past the synagogue, whose dome was ablaze. Fear went right through me. A big crowd of people stood around it silently and the fire department was content with protecting the surrounding houses from catching fire. My way took me to the Jewish school, where I got out to check on my children. There they still did not know about the burning House of Worship, and only in the factory did I hear through telephone reports that all Jewish businesses in the city were completely demolished. The wares were thrown onto the street and set on fire, and all this happened at the hands of only a few juveniles who had been appointed by the party for this purpose."[160]

✡ Like Carnival ✡

Virtually no town or synagogue was spared. In Wittlich, a small village in the Mosel Valley in western Germany, the SA destroyed the synagogue too. "The intricate lead crystal window above the door crashed into the street and pieces of furniture came flying through doors and windows. A shouting SA man climbed to the roof waving the rolls of the Torah: 'Wipe your asses with it, Jews!' he screamed while he hurled them like bands of confetti on Karnival."[161]

✡ Look at the Red Sky ✡

Around midnight on November 9, Henry Oertelt remembered his mother drawing the curtains and then suddenly calling him and his brother over to the window. "'Just look at that red sky! There must be a fire nearby,' she uttered with a hint of amazement in her voice. We waited to hear sirens of fire engines, but there were none. When all remained quiet we said 'good night' and went to bed. Wondering why the sky was so red, we fell asleep.

"The next morning I bicycled as usual to my workplace, my furniture workshop. Suddenly I could ride no further and had to climb off my bike! I was forced to pick it up and carry it with its crossbar on my shoulder. I carefully wove my way through the shards of shattered glass that were strewn everywhere. The few Jewish-owned stores in the neighborhood had been ransacked and demolished. Parts of their now damaged merchandise mingled here and there with the splintered fragments of their once shiny display shelves. My eyes surveyed the destruction with disbelief. I tried, without much success, to avoid crunching on the broken glass.

"A few blocks away, the inside of my family's synagogue had been completely demolished. All the holy items had been trampled on and torn into pieces. All windows, some of them made of beautiful stained glass, had been smashed. There was nothing but glass wherever I stepped. Later on, I learned that the building itself had been spared from being burned because some private non-Jewish-owned apartment houses were too dangerously close to its structure."[162]

✡ What a Racket ✡

In the village of Baisingen, home to only 80 Jews, the residents witnessed the destruction of the synagogue and the general mayhem of the SA: "On November 9, 1938, between 10 and 11 in the evening, I was sitting at home and heard a loud noise coming from somewhere very close to my apartment. So I went outside into the street and immediately noted that the racket was coming from the synagogue. On approaching the synagogue, I observed that there were some 50 to 60 people both within the building and outside. I also noticed that various persons were likewise in the homes of the Jews in the vicinity. I could hear from outside the awful din and commotion inside the synagogue, and that everything was being smashed to pieces. I was able to notice too that some books and other objects had been taken out of the synagogue and were then set on fire nearby behind the Jewish house of Friedrich Kahn. I also saw the Tala scrolls [Torah] being carried out of the synagogue and then burned by one of the men."[163]

✡ A Heap of Ruins ✡

A synagogue official in Potsdam was arrested at 5:30 a.m. and later taken to the synagogue where he was asked by one of the Nazis to show him the Holy of Holies. "By now, the mob at the front gate of the synagogue had pushed its way in. A fearful scene was played out with uncanny speed. In a few minutes the whole interior of the synagogue was transformed into a heap of ruins. All the windows were smashed with wooden hand grenades, as used in army training, all the chandeliers were torn down, the benches were chopped up, the women's gallery demolished, the Rabbi's seat and the warden's box hacked to pieces, the curtains torn down, the Scrolls of the Law ripped into shreds, the great Menorah used as a battering ram. Nothing was left unharmed.

"It was so terrible and bestial that the leader of the group—certainly no soft-hearted person—said to me, 'We'd better go.'

"As we left I saw small tongues of flames licking their way upwards in the foyer. Later I heard that the postal authorities had raised a vigorous protest against any conflagration involving the synagogue. This was not because of any humane considerations . . . but because any fire would have endangered the large post office adjacent to the synagogue."[164]

✡ The Only Complaint ✡

In a trial in Wiesbaden, the destruction of the synagogue in Rüdesheim was described in detail. The defendant received an order by telephone at approximately 2 a.m. on November 10 to destroy the synagogues in his area, but his men were not to wear any uniforms. Four men entered the synagogue and removed all the prayer books and documents and then poured gasoline inside the building. When they threw a burning piece of paper on the gasoline, an explosion threw one man against the entrance of the synagogue. A second man's coat caught fire. Awakened by the noise, several nearby residents came and found the chairs smoldering, charred Torah scrolls on the floor, and other debris. Later the district attorney sent a note to the police stating his "displeasure that Rüdesheim had been the only community to file a complaint on the burning of the synagogue."[165]

✡ Private Property ✡

Kate Freyhan was a teacher at the Jewish girls' school and lived opposite the synagogue in Tiergarten. When she returned home from work on November 10, she saw schoolchildren throwing rocks at the synagogue. The police stood and watched as the children carried on their attack throughout the afternoon. One woman expressed a typical German sentiment when she told Freyhan that it was disgraceful the way the police stood by and did nothing because "it is private property."[166]

✡ Dancing around the Fire ✡

Rabbi Max Eschelbacher had been arrested in Düsseldorf on Kristallnacht. Later, he went to the synagogue and found the windows smashed and the roof burned. "During the night of the pogrom, a band of men had showed up there. . . . The scrolls of the Torah were removed from the *Aron Hakodesh* (Torah shrine) and set afire in the yard. The murdering arsonists danced in a circle around the burning scrolls, some of them wearing the robes of the rabbis and *chazanim* (cantors).

"Then everything made of wood, especially the roof truss and the benches, were covered with gasoline and tar and set on fire. Soon the roof truss was burning brightly. This is how our synagogue was burned down. Other synagogues were blown up. The mortuary at our old cemetery was destroyed."[167]

CHAPTER 7

Righteous Germans

The actions on Kristallnacht were carried out by a small minority of the citizens in Germany and Austria. Few may have been perpetrators, but the vast majority were bystanders who could have objected to what they knew was a government-sanctioned pogrom against their fellow citizens, or could have intervened to protect their neighbors. The willingness of so many to join either the group of perpetrators or bystanders undoubtedly encouraged Hitler to believe he could expel and, ultimately, exterminate the Jews. Over the next seven years, most of the people of Germany and the other countries that came under Hitler's thumb would prove he was correct. Still, on Kristallnacht, as well as during the war, a few people stood up for what was right and did speak out or intervene.

- In Sontheim a Christian coal merchant took out a gun and used it to drive away the Nazis who were preparing to set the synagogue on fire. He then escorted Jews out of town before they could be arrested.[168]
- Cardinal Michael von Faulhaber provided a truck for the chief rabbi of Munich to save religious objects from the synagogue before it was destroyed.

- Former world heavyweight boxing champion Max Schmeling hid two sons of a Jewish clothing store owner in his Berlin hotel suite. He stayed in his room pretending to be ill for four days until he heard it was safe for the boys to leave.[169]
- When the Gestapo prepared to set Berlin's Oranienburger Strasse synagogue on fire, the local police chief, Wilhelm Krützfeld, told them the building was a historic landmark. Krützfeld was reprimanded for his intervention. He saved the synagogue from arson, but it was ultimately destroyed when the British bombed the city in 1943.
- A British reporter witnessed the unusual action of two German army officers preventing a mob from destroying a Jewish shop in Berlin. They were threatened by the crowd and forced to retreat. The reporter said the two men "seemed to be the only persons left in the Reich who dared to stand up for decency and restraint."[170]

✡ Catholic Piety ✡

A few Jews lived in the small village of Warmsried in southern Swabia, situated in the Alps. The town was dominated by a Catholic priest named Father Andreas Rampp. The priest did not support the Nazi Party and the village had few members. No one was allowed to join the SA; anyone who wanted to had to go elsewhere. None of the party celebrations were permitted, and the swastika was not even allowed to be displayed. On Kristallnacht no actions were taken against the Jews, partly because of Rampp and partly because the village's economy depended on a sawmill that was run by a Jew who had been driven out of another town. That Jew stayed in Warmsried for the entire war and survived. Two other villages, Derching and Laimering in Bavaria, also did not allow any attacks on their Jewish residents.[171]

✡ The Maid Repays ✡

Inge Berner left her job in Berlin after receiving a warning "that they're killing Jews all over Berlin" from the bookkeeper. "I went home on back streets and my father was there. Then our former maid came and said, 'Come with me and I will hide you.' My father didn't want to. But then people started calling and he heard what was going on and he went. My father had stayed with this woman and her husband for about a week."[172]

✡ Come Back Later ✡

Siegfried Buchwalter lived in a Vienna apartment house that had three Jewish stores on the first floor: a tinsmith, a shoemaker, and a gourmet grocery. When his father returned from the synagogue, they were told Brownshirts were breaking into stores, smashing windows and stealing things. Siegfried saw Hitler Youth and Brownshirts viciously beat a man. "They saw me and knew me. I locked the door. Then my father came out. These Hitler Youth had a gun and threatened my father with a gun to open the door. Then a non-Jewish lady, a Czech, came down. She lived on the third floor and we lived on the second. She asked, 'What do you want?' They said they wanted me. She said, 'When you come back with the brownshirts you can get him.' They left and she hid me in her house."[173]

✡ That Was My Aunt ✡

Frank Correl recalled his father going to the Gestapo office in Frankfurt am Main to get a passport and exit visa. "A functionary asked if he was Mr. Cohen who owned the Wagner and Schertle store and he said, 'Yes, I am.' He said, 'Do you remember a customer by the name of such and such—a woman?'

"This is when my father got very scared because he thought it was going to be part of this sexual harassment business. And he said, 'Yes, I do.'

"The Gestapo official said, 'Do you remember that you would take her out in your car from time to time?'

"My father said, 'Yes, I do.'

"The Gestapo agent said, 'Why did you do that?'

"My father said, 'The lady was handicapped. She was a good customer. I wanted to do something for her to show my appreciation and to make her feel better. That's why, on Sundays, I occasionally offered her a ride into the nice countryside outside of Frankfurt.'

"And the Gestapo official got up and said, 'That was my aunt. Here is your passport.'"

Correl said his father later received a tip that he should get out of Germany. That allowed him to escape just hours before the pogrom began. "To the best of my knowledge, the tip came from the same person," Correl added. His father went first to South Africa and then, fearing he would be interned, continued on to Mozambique. "I didn't know where he was or when he'd come back."[174]

✡ Teaching a Lesson ✡

Lotte Kramer went to hide in her attic with one of her friends and her mother when they heard a mob approaching their street in Mainz. From their hiding place they could peek out the window and watch as the hooligans ransacked the home of the Jewish widow across the way. Suddenly, they heard the voice of the headmaster of the boy's high school shouting at the vandals, "The Führer will not stand for this kind of behavior!"

The reprimand worked, and the crowd left without further incident. Later, however, Lotte met one of her teachers who had just left the home of the headmaster of the Jewish school and reported that he and his wife had gassed themselves. Apparently a group of students from the school where he had taught for many years before being forced to leave had attacked his home.[175]

✡ No Threat to the Reich ✡

The Gestapo came to the Berlin home of two-year-old Hannelore Heinemann looking for her father and grandfather. The two men had already gone into hiding, so the Nazis promptly left. They returned later, but were stopped in the hall by the building's concierge, Frau Müller, who told the agents the men no longer lived there. 'Take my word for it,' she told them. 'Only his wife and daughter remain. Why do you want to disturb a young woman and a two-year-old child? Surely they are not a threat to the Reich.'"[176] The Gestapo left and did not return again.

✡ Taking a Stand ✡

After storm troopers had broken into 12-year-old Lucie Draschler's Vienna home and taken away her father, a gentile neighbor who lived on the same floor came over and insisted that Lucie and her sister stay with her. Draschler said she hardly knew the elderly woman, who lived with her sister and brother, but they stayed in the apartment until the following day. "When they witnessed what went on, they decided to take a stand and help. They fussed over us, talked to us, kept feeding us, and were so kind to us, that we slowly recovered."[177]

✡ Diplomatic Intervention ✡

In some cases, the people who stood up to the Nazis or acted to save Jews were not Germans, but foreigners, often diplomats. The wife of the Brazilian vice-consul, Carmen de Carvalho, helped Hugo Levy escape the Nazis in Hamburg. First, she hid him in the consulate, then she obtained the documents he and his wife needed to immigrate to Brazil. Then she personally drove them in her husband's official car to the dock to meet the ship that would take them to safety.[178]

✡ Safe in a Nursing Home ✡

Richard Fuchs learned that Jews were being arrested in Berlin and decided to go into hiding. "My wife was ill at a nursing home in Baden-Baden, and I took a third-class sleeper in a night train. The train was searched during the night without my noticing it; every Jew found there travelling away from his home was arrested. That I escaped arrest is almost a miracle. In Baden-Baden I found myself the only male Jew at liberty; the generous head of my wife's nursing home allowed me to hide there for a time."[179]

✡ The Care of a Caretaker ✡

Eighteen-year-old Charlotte Neumann was studying at a teacher's training seminary in Würzburg when the caretaker came in at 2:00 a.m. Charlotte and her roommates saw that he was dressed in his SA uniform and didn't know what to expect. The man told the girls to get dressed and run away because "they" were destroying the synagogue and attacking Jewish homes and shops. The girls escaped to the nearby woods.

Neumann returned to the seminary 23 years later. She came with her daughter who was the same age as Charlotte had been on *Kristallnacht*. To her surprise, the caretaker was still there. At one point she shouted at him, "You Germans are all the same. Everything happened by itself and Hitler did it singlehandedly." He responded, "If you were really here that night, you know what I did." Charlotte broke down and apologized.[180]

✡ No Jews Live Here ✡

Because of simple acts of kindness Jews were often spared on Kristallnacht. In Leipzig 14-year-old Esther Reisz lived in an apartment with a non-Jewish housekeeper. When the Nazis began their rampage through the neighborhood, the woman would not let them enter the building. "I remember standing behind the curtain shivering with fright, and we heard the housekeeper shout to the Nazis, 'Go away. No Jews live here.'"[181]

The Schemel family had a similar experience in Berlin. They were forced to move from a nice home to a smaller flat, but still couldn't afford it without renting out a room to a man who turned out to be a member of the SA. On Kristallnacht, a mob came for the Schemels, and the Nazi stuck his head out the window and shouted, "Go away! There are no Jews here!" Luckily, the man's brown shirt had convinced them he was telling the truth. "I am in the SA," he told the Schemels later, "but I don't like what is going on here." Still, the man moved out shortly afterward.[182]

✡ Preventing a Crime ✡

At the Nuremberg Trials after the war, Nazis would famously declare they were "just following orders" when they carried out their crimes against humanity. It was possible for Germans to disobey orders, however, and many did despite the perceived risks. Nazi official Wichard von Bredow, for example, was ordered to burn down the synagogue in the East Prussian town of Schirwindt. He put on his army uniform and told his wife as he walked out the door of his home, "I'm going to the synagogue in Schirwindt where I want to prevent one of the greatest crimes in my district." When the arsonists from the SA and other Nazis arrived at the synagogue, von Bredow was waiting for them with his revolver. The group left and the synagogue was saved, the only one in the district that survived. Despite his act of disobedience, von Bredow was not punished and remained the county officer throughout the war.[183]

✡ Devotion and Guilt ✡

Sometimes the reaction of Germans to the pogrom was not particularly dramatic but consisted of simple kindnesses that meant a great deal to the traumatized Jews. Mally Dienemann recalled the kind actions of her non-Jewish landlady in Offenbach am Main: "Her devotion and guilt . . . knew no bounds. These simple people . . . brought me flowers when I was alone . . . and other Jews must have also known such people in one form or another. For officially we were all supposed to starve during these November days."[184]

✡ Look and Never Forget ✡

"November 9th was also my father's birthday," Edith Reisfeld recalled. She was 10 years old when the Nazis came to their apartment in Wiesbaden. Her family owned a business in the same building, and they were awakened that night by the sound of glass shattering in the store. "My parents must have realized immediately what was happening. And we all got dressed very quickly." The house had a cellar, and her father and a relative visiting from Frankfurt went inside to hide. "My mother and myself went to the back of the store because at that point, they were in the front. And there was a room in the back store and she opened the door and . . . we fled the building. I remember it was dark. I remember we hid in a large doorway because you could hear the sirens, probably the police sirens. And somewhere along that point my parents must have made a decision where to run to. The young man decided to split and try and get back to Frankfurt to his own family.

My parents and myself, we made it to a home of Germans, not Jews, Germans. They knew my parents. Probably they'd done business with them, I don't know. My parents sought shelter and wanted to spend the night. The family had a son who was a Brownshirt. Unless he gave permission for us to remain there over the night, they couldn't do anything, so we sat and waited for him to come. . . . Now when I think about it, he might have been only 17 or 18, but our lives depended on whether he gave permission for us to spend the night. And he did.

The next morning my father took me to a window and he showed me in the distance, because where we were staying was

higher up in the city, and you could look down onto that synagogue, the Michelsbecks synagogue. It was on fire. I remember
he put his arm around me and I started to cry. He said to me, 'I
want you to look and never to forget what happened.' And I still
remember that today."[185]

✡ Tailor-Made Help ✡

Bernt Engelmann was to report to the Luftwaffe (German air force)
when violence broke out in Düsseldorf. He witnessed a group of
Nazis ransacking the apartment of a Jewish family that lived in
his building. Engelmann reluctantly went inside and succeeded
in stopping them from stealing a candelabra and convinced them
to leave. In the meantime, his mother had taken in the little Jewish girl who lived there and told Bernt to go out and find her parents. When he located them, they were frantic until he reassured
them their daughter was safe. After hearing about the destruction in their flat, the father asked if Bernt knew if anything had
happened to a painting they owned. The man said, "I put all the
money we had into it. It's 'degenerate art'—*that* you're allowed to
take with you. We want to sell it over there and use the money to
make a new start." Bernt didn't know what painting he was talking about until he heard the description. It was a Chagall. Bernt
told him it was damaged, but he thought it could be repaired.
Bernt also promised to take the painting to his apartment and
make sure no one stole it. He then escorted the husband and wife

to the home of an Aryan family they knew who agreed to let them stay the night.

"Back home, I fetched the painting from my apartment and hid it under my bed. Then I set out again, this time with my bicycle. On Sternstrasse I braked just in time to avoid an entire X-ray machine that came hurtling out of a second-floor window. A heat lamp hit the sidewalk with a loud crash, and all sorts of instruments came raining down after it.

"From Sternstrasse I bicycled into the center of town. All the Jewish stores with which I was familiar presented the same picture: smashed windows, vandalized interiors, the goods plundered or tossed out onto the street—it seemed to have made no difference whether they were stockings or fur coats.

"Some distance away I saw the glow of fire against the sky. It was the Kasernenstrasse synagogue, which had fallen victim to 'a spontaneous outbreak of the people's rage,' as we heard over the radio the next day. In actuality, the 'people,' of whom only a few were about at this late hour, were horrified at this act of barbarism. The police and firemen stood by without lifting a finger. . . . On Steinstrasse I encountered a woman with a little child. The woman cowered against the wall of a building when she caught sight of my bicycle headlight, but the child jerked away from her and began to cry. I stopped and asked whether I could help. She gave me a look full of hate, and pulled the child close to her.

"'We've had plenty of help this evening,' she said bitterly. 'Please leave us alone and—' She broke off as loud male voices could be heard approaching.

"I came up close to her and whispered, 'Don't be afraid.' I put my arm around her; she was completely rigid. The child was quiet now, huddled in the shadows. Four men in high boots and civilian clothes passed us, talking and laughing loudly.

"'I'm taking the day off tomorrow,' one of them said. 'I've put in a hard night.'

"The others laughed raucously. One of them yelled a coarse remark at us, whom they took for a pair of lovers; and they laughed again but didn't stop. A few minutes later they were out of sight and the street was quiet once more.

"'Thank you,' the woman said as I took my arm from her shoulder. 'Excuse me for thinking that of you....'"

Bernt asked if she had a place to stay and she said, "Not anymore," so he led her to a nearby shop where he knew the proprietor, Herr Desch, had an apartment upstairs. When the shop owner opened the door, it was almost 2:30 a.m., but he was fully dressed and thought that Bernt had come to pick up his uniform. When he saw the woman and child, he let them inside and locked the door behind them. "'It's a bit crowded,' he said in his normal voice, and showed us into the shop. In the workroom, in the pressing room, and even between the fabric racks in the back of the shop people were sitting or lying. Some had fallen asleep; others were talking in low voices. Some were still so much in shock that they did not even look up when we entered.

"'In the kitchenette over there you'll find hot tea and milk,' Herr Desch told the woman and child, 'and in the room behind it, there's still some space. That should do for now, and tomorrow . . . we'll have to see.'. . . He led me into the darkened showroom. In the pale light shining from the half-opened workroom door I glimpsed an SS officer's uniform on a dummy.

"'The injured ones are upstairs in our apartment, with my wife and Fräulein Bonse,' he said softly. 'The doctor has been here already. I still have no idea what to do with all these people. There are too many of them—someone is bound to notice.'"[186]

CHAPTER 8

Taking Lives

In addition to the rampant destruction of Jewish homes, businesses, and houses of worship on Kristallnacht, some roaming mobs of Nazis went so far as to commit murder. Goebbels received the report of the first death in Munich around 2:00 a.m. He reportedly responded by saying curtly, don't "get so worked up about the death of a Jew. In the next days, thousands more would kick the bucket."[187]

The German Ministry of Justice issued a ruling that the destruction of synagogues, cemeteries, and other Jewish property should not be prosecuted unless the destruction was committed for the purpose of looting. The ministry also said the murder or physical abuse of Jews should only be prosecuted if the act had been perpetrated solely "for selfish reasons."[188]

Susanne Stern, an 81-year-old widow, was murdered in Eberstadt by SA officer Adolf Heinrich Frey. In 1940 he was brought to trial by the German Ministry of Justice, and Frey coldly described his actions: "I knocked on the door. . . . I demanded that Stern get dressed. She sat down on the . . . sofa. When I asked her whether she did not intend to follow my instructions and get dressed, she answered she would not get dressed or come with us. We can do whatever we want. . . . 'I am not leaving my house. I am an old lady.' . . . I took my service revolver out of my pocket. . . . I called on the woman another 5 or 6 times to get up and dress. Stern loudly screamed into my face with scorn and insolence: 'I will not get up and I will not get dressed. You can do with me whatever you want.' At the moment she screamed, 'Do with me whatever you want.' I released the safety of the pistol and shot her once. . . . Stern collapsed on the sofa. She leaned back and grabbed her chest with her hands. I now shot her for the second time, this time aiming at her head." Frey's case was dismissed.[189]

At 2:30 a.m. members of the SS in the picturesque town of Innsbruck, Austria, gathered and were given the order by their commander, Oberführer Hanns von Feil, "to kill the Jews on Gänsbacher Strasse silently." The head of the Jewish community, Richard Berger, was dragged out of his house in his pajamas and put in a car. Berger thought he was being taken to Gestapo headquarters but soon realized the car was not headed in that direction. He asked where he was being taken but didn't receive an answer. When they came to the Inn River, Berger was dragged out of the car, beaten, and thrown in the river. He died. Another Innsbruck Jew, Karl Bauer, was dragged out of his apartment and beaten. He died on the way to the hospital. A third man, Richard Graubart, was stabbed to death in front of his wife and daughter.[190]

In Germany, Rabbi Max Eschelbacher learned after being released from prison in Düsseldorf that a number of people had been murdered on Kristallnacht. Paul Marcus, the proprietor of a café was shot. Mrs. Isidor Willner and her son Ernst were stabbed to death in Hilden. Carl Herz and Nathan Mayer were either shot or stabbed.[191]

In Nuremberg nine Jews were murdered including Jacob Spaeth, who was beaten to death; Paul Lebrecht, who was thrown from the window of his shop; Paul Astruck, who was found mutilated in the woods, and Nathan Langstadt, whose throat was cut.[192]

Men broke into the Lowenthal home in Aschaffenburg, a large Bavarian town situated along the Main River, and shot and killed Ludwig Lowenthal in his bed. His brother-in-law, Alfons Vogel, was kidnapped and taken to the woods where he was tied to a tree and used for target practice. He, too, was killed.[193]

The Berlin correspondent of the *Daily Telegraph* reported that the caretaker of the Prinzregenstrasse Synagogue and his family were burned to death and that four Jews were lynched.[194]

At the time of the Nazi takeover in 1933, more than 1,000 Jews lived in the town of Bremen in northwestern Germany. Five were killed on Kristallnacht, including Selma Zwienicki, who was shot and killed in her home by storm troopers when she refused to reveal the whereabouts of her husband.[195]

Fewer than 100 Jews lived in the northwestern German town of Beckum. On Kristallnacht the synagogue and school were destroyed along with Jewish stores and homes. Jews were assaulted, and at least one, 95-year-old Alexander Falek, was murdered.[196]

In the small German horse-trading town of Jastrow (now the Polish town of Jastrowie), Max Freundlich was one of about 125 Jews. Married and the father of three children, he died while being arrested on November 9. The synagogue in town was destroyed, Jewish businesses were demolished, and the men were taken to Sachsenhausen.[197]

Glogau was a Nazi stronghold, but it is now in Poland. In the 1930s, the town had about 500 Jews. One of them, Leonhard Ferdinand Plachte, was killed when he was thrown from a window.[198]

The SA commander in Lesum, a small village near Bremen, announced, "By tonight, there must be no Jews left in Germany. The Jewish shops must also be destroyed." Very few Jews lived in the town, but the local members of the SA believed they had their marching orders and proceeded to kill a Mr. and Mrs. Goldberg and a man named Sinsohn.[199]

Among the others who lost their lives during Kristallnacht was Leopold Schoen in Vienna.[200]

Jews rarely offered resistance to their attackers since they were unarmed and typically faced groups of men who had sticks, knives, iron bars, guns, and other weapons. One exception was in the wine-making center of Heilbronn, Germany, where a Jewish family threw an SA attacker out of the window. In the German city of Hilden, however, a Jew and his mother were killed with an ax on a chopping block after trying to fight back. Another Jew was stabbed to death after he tried to resist.[201]

✡ No Way Out ✡

Many Jews saw no way out and took their own lives. The British consul general, A. E. Dowden, lived in Frankfurt am Main and witnessed "scenes of indescribable, destructive sadism and brutality." He reported that 11 acquaintances had taken their own lives to escape arrest. Several other Jews were found hanging from trees in the woods just outside the city.[202]

Not far from Frankfurt, in the town of Würzburg, three women killed themselves after their husbands were arrested. One swallowed poison, a second drowned herself in the Main River, and the third jumped out of a window.[203]

The Engelhards owned the only Jewish laundry in Munich. On Kristallnacht, when the Nazis came to the business, they did not vandalize it. They told Mr. Engelhard to finish his deliveries and then hand over the keys. Bertha Engelhard recalled seeing her father after he'd returned. "Father came home ashen-faced, because one of the customers he had gone to deliver laundry to had committed suicide, both he and his wife."[204]

Many other suicides were recorded:

- Ten people killed themselves in Nuremberg.[205]
- In Munich the man who had managed the fortune of the Bavarian royal family, Emil Kraemer, jumped out of the window with his wife when the Gestapo came to arrest him.[206]
- Dr. Bernhard Rosenthal, a gynecologist in Frankfurt am Main, committed suicide.
- In Cologne 200 people hid in the cellar of a hospital. Many of these were patients who had attempted suicide. Some were allowed to die.[207]
- Martin Cobliner was a music teacher in Hamburg. He committed suicide on November 10, when the Gestapo came to arrest him.[208]
- Josephine Baehr, a married mother of two, was part of a tiny Jewish community in Bassum. She committed suicide when the Nazis came to arrest her husband and then demolished her home.[209]

- In Vienna perhaps as many as 30 people committed suicide, including Professor Philip Freud, a sexagenarian relative of Sigmund Freud who had been beaten up in his bed.[210]
- In the Austrian town of Ingolstadt, the mayor reported that "a local Jewish couple drowned themselves in the Danube."[211]

"Those who mourned the suicides did not criticize or pity them," Lionel Kaplan noted. "They rarely condemned them for flouting religious proscriptions against suicide. Nor did the mourners blame those who died for leaving the living more desolate than ever. . . . Those reflecting on the suicides of relatives or friends often admired the courage it took to end one's own life." To illustrate this frame of mind, Kaplan cites Nora Rosenthal as understanding that her husband couldn't take the strain of Nazi persecution, even though she was left with the responsibility of escaping from Germany with her two children.[212]

✡ Seeking Shelter ✡

As the situation for Jews in Germany deteriorated, more and more people began to look for ways out of the country. Following Kristallnacht thousands were desperate to emigrate. In fact, most who were imprisoned in concentration camps were told that promising to leave Germany was their only way to gain release. At that time, the camps were not functioning as extermination centers. Many men still died from the conditions and abuse, but the Nazis' intent was to stimulate a Jewish exodus. Even those who escaped imprisonment finally understood that there was no future for Jews in Germany and looked for a haven. By that time, however, it was already getting to be too late, as few countries were willing to accept Jews, and the Nazis had cancelled the passports of all German Jews a month before Kristallnacht and required them to reapply for new documents marked with a J to identify them as Jews.

Yitzhak Herz, the man in charge at the orphanage in Dinslaken, described the onerous process involved in emigrating:

> *Jews wishing to leave the German Reich had to fill out endless application forms. They had to go to or write to many offices. There were precise instructions concerning which belongings one was allowed to take out of the country. A list of all items had to be affixed on the inside of every valise. The order applied to everyone, adult and child.*
>
> *A former Jewish employee, preparing to emigrate, had to prove to the authorities that he had paid all his taxes in full. The forms had to be sent to the police of the district in which the potential emigrant was living. The next job was to obtain a health certificate from a Jewish physician. A Jew was allowed to consult only a Jewish doctor, officially licensed by the Nazi authorities. . . . The reader would be wrong to assume, however, that these four forms in Photostat were sufficient to obtain an official passport. Every Jew had to have a so-called Kennkarte (identity card), stamped with a "J" clearly*

indicating that the holder was a Jew or Jewess. In the top right-hand corner was a fingerprint of the index finger. Each card was numbered. Even small children were obliged to have identity cards.[213]

In late 1938 and early 1939, 50,000 Jews fled Germany.

Just four months before Kristallnacht, a conference with delegates from 32 countries met at Evian, France, to discuss what to do about the growing number of refugees trying to flee Europe. The United States, which had initially proposed the conference, showed so little interest in solving the problem that other countries felt no need to open their doors to fleeing Jews. After the conference, Rabbi Leo Baeck told C. Brooks Peters, an American reporter in Berlin, "The future is dim. No one wants us."[214]

In the end, the Dominican Republic was the only country that participated at the Evian Conference that welcomed Jews. Though the island offered to take in 100,000 Jews, only 5,000 visas were issued and only 645 Jews went to the island.

One of the few other places to accept large numbers of Jews was Shanghai, largely because of the courageous efforts of a Chinese diplomat in the consulate in Vienna. Dr. Feng Shan Ho issued thousands of visas, and 18,000 Jews ultimately reached safety in Shanghai.

Still, more than half of Germany's Jews managed to immigrate to the United States and Great Britain between 1933 and September 1939, when the Germans invaded Poland. More than 40,000 reached Palestine, but the numbers declined precipitously after the Arabs began their revolt against the authorities in 1936. The British hoped to assuage Arab anger by slowing Jewish immigration to Palestine.

Jews who subsequently attempted to illegally enter Palestine to escape Hitler were seized and imprisoned in detention centers.

Great Britain agreed to accept 25,000 refugees, including some 7,000 Jewish children. These Jews came through the "Kindertransports," which began with 206 German children who had fled with a day's notice to England via a ship leaving from Holland. These children were taken care of by British families. Holocaust historian Leni Yahil noted this was not entirely an altruistic gesture. "The British government acted less out of a humanitarian impulse," she said, "than a desire to avoid pressures to admit more Jews to Palestine."[215] In addition, officials hoped to avoid inflaming the situation in Palestine where the Jews and ruling British mandatory authorities already had a tense relationship.

Jews had also met with Prime Minister Neville Chamberlain and asked him to permit a limited number of children and teenagers to enter the country for agricultural training with the promise they would be resettled outside Britain. The proposal was ultimately rejected as Chamberlain insisted that anything he might do to intervene in Germany might worsen the situation of the Jews.

The Jewish officials in Germany responsible for emigration to Palestine also did everything possible to help Jews escape from Germany. The Gestapo even requested officials in the Berlin Palestine office double their efforts, but most of the organization's offices had been shut down or destroyed and many of the employees were imprisoned in concentration camps.

Ruben Golan hid in a seminary for Jewish kindergarten teachers on Kristallnacht. After the arrest of the leader of *Hechalutz* (an association of Jewish youth training its members to settle in Palestine),

Golan took over managing the organization and immediately sent permits to all members of the group, certifying that they were to be admitted to England, Sweden, and Holland. "I sent out about 1,000 such permits, which were sufficient to secure the release of their holders from the concentration camps. Very soon we did the same for the members of the Youth Aliyah; this scheme proved successful. We sent out more permits than in fact had been granted at that time."[216]

The place most Jews hoped to immigrate to was the United States, the country that stood for freedom, whose welcoming symbol, the Statue of Liberty, was emblazoned with the words of the Jewish poet Emma Lazarus: "Give me your tired, your poor, / Your huddled masses yearning to breathe free, / The wretched refuse of your teeming shore. / Send these, the homeless, tempest-tost to me, / I lift my lamp beside the golden door!"

The United States admitted 200,000 refugees—the largest number accepted by any country—but the American response to the catastrophe that was beginning to engulf the Jews was still woefully inadequate. The reasons for the failure to accept more of the people fleeing persecution from Europe were concerns about the economy, anti-Semitism, and xenophobia. On November 20, 1938, President Franklin D. Roosevelt agreed to allow German refugees already in the United States on visitors' visas to remain because he said it would be "cruel and inhuman" to send them back to be persecuted in Germany. This act saved as many as 15,000 Jews, but he could have done far more and undoubtedly would have saved tens of thousands more if he had pushed for an increase in the immigration quota, combined the annual quota for German and Austrian immigrants, or perhaps given the Jews a special exemption (in 1940 Roosevelt sent a list of 200 names to the State Department with instructions for them to be given emergency visas).[217]

The United States was just coming out of the Great Depression, and Americans favored an isolationist policy that would keep them out of the type of foreign entanglements that had led to the Great War. They were also concerned that a flood of refugees would threaten the recovery and be a drag on the economy. The nation also had a strong undercurrent of anti-Semitism, which increased the reluctance of the government to offer specific aid to Jews. This sentiment was further exacerbated by a general distrust of foreigners, feelings that persisted even in this great nation of immigrants.

The American public felt sympathy for the victims of Kristallnacht, but this did not translate into support for allowing more Jews into the United States. A poll by the National Opinion Research Center in Chicago, for example, found that 94 percent disapproved of the Nazi treatment of Jews, but 72 percent were opposed to admitting a large number of German Jews to the United States. Two-thirds of the American public opposed legislation that would have permitted 20,000 Jewish children to enter the United States on an emergency basis. The bill died in the Senate in 1939 after opponents argued that the Jewish children would flood orphanages, that it wasn't fair to help foreign children at the expense of American ones, that Nazi or Communist children might slip in and that a precedent would be set for making exceptions to quotas for other countries, and that this would open the door to demands later that the parents be admitted as well.[218]

Survivor after survivor recounts efforts to get to the United States. Tens of thousands were on a waiting list, but the numbers indicating their position were hardly worth the paper they were printed on.

"Our visa number for the United States was 41,000 something and we weren't going to get to the U.S. anytime soon," recalled Frank Correl.[219] Similarly, Ernest Michel recalled being told in 1938 he could go to the United States in 1942, that is, four years later.[220]

Alfred Kleeman's brother, Sigi, in a twist of fate, had gone to Stuttgart on Kristallnacht to get his visa from the American consul. "He was also already preparing for immigration. So, everything went well at the Consul, and he received his visa, but on that day and that afternoon, things began to happen with the destruction of all the Jewish homes and properties. So he called my parents from Stuttgart to ask what he should do. So my parents told him, 'Don't come home. Take your visa, and go directly to your cousin. Take a train and go directly to Basle.' That's on the German border in Switzerland. And they told him, 'Don't dare come home.' On the strength of the American visa that he had in his pocket, he was allowed to enter Switzerland because they knew he wasn't staying, that his objective was only to temporarily wait out his time there. Meanwhile, he had a ticket booked on the *SS Washington*. Under normal circumstances he would have come home, said goodbye, and gone by train to Hamburg to board that ship for America. But under the circumstances, with what was happening, he could not do that. So the next best thing he could do was go to Basle, which he did. The same ship, the *SS Washington*, also made a stop in Le Havre, on the French coast. So he went by train to Le Havre, and was able to board the ship for America."[221]

Edward Adler had been arrested in June and sent to a concentration camp for three months prior to Kristallnacht. "When I came out of the concentration camp, I had to report to the Gestapo. Ten o'clock every morning, except Sundays, you had to go downtown. They want to be sure I'm still all right, that I wasn't sick, you know, they wanted to take good care of me. Kristallnacht happened on November 9th. November the 10th, in the morning, we stayed at my mother's, and my wife says, 'I'll go downtown with you.' We went downtown, we got on a streetcar, and there was all kinds of commotion. What's going on, we didn't know. We hadn't put a radio on or anything. We got downtown and there were a million people. The city of Hamburg had three million people, it was a very large city, and in the finest stores, the finest Jewish stores, the windows were smashed, and the mannequins were laying on the street, and people were burning books and dancing around it. I turned up my collar, I'll never forget, and put my head down, and said, 'God, if somebody should recognize me, I'll be torn to pieces.'

"We went to the Gestapo building, and there were lots of people loitering outside on the first floor. I said to my wife, 'Run upstairs and see what's going on.' We had no idea. She ran upstairs. I don't think she ever ran a flight of stairs so fast in her entire life. She came down. I was hiding in a basement of the building across the street. She came over and said, 'They're all going to be arrested again. You have to get out of here.'

"We went to the Holland/America cruise line, where we already had re-made reservations to come to this country because my wife took care of all that while I was still in camp, but we didn't have the money to pay for the tickets anymore because it was all confiscated. My father-in-law, who was well-established in business, had nothing left. My wife called a very famous banker with the name of Walberg. He called the Holland/America line and guaranteed payments for the tickets."[222]

After Fritzi Bellamy's mother learned her father was in Dachau, she tried to find out if there was a way of getting him out. "She was told you'll sign over all your belongings and you'll get a visa for an overseas country for him, yourself and your daughter and we will let him out and you will leave within 36 hours. The first thing we had to do was to sign everything over to get valid passports. We signed everything and got passports with a big 'J' stamped in them. We tried to get an American visa but we couldn't. We realized the big mistake my father had made was not to register in the beginning but he registered later on. Mother phoned Belgium and spoke to her cousin who was married to the Romanian consul's daughter. They got in touch with the Romanian consul who said, 'Mail those passports immediately.' He had a connection with someone who worked for the embassy of Uruguay and got a visa for us to go to Uruguay."[223]

Eugene Garbaty owned one of Germany's largest cigar factories until he was imprisoned in the Sachsenhausen concentration camp and was forced to sell it for one million marks, one-tenth of its value. He then was fined one-half million marks and had to use the other half million marks to bribe Berlin's police chief to obtain an exit visa.[224]

George Ginsburg's parents were devastated by Kristallnacht. "We had to get out. My parents were trying to save me so they made applications. I had an uncle, the brother of my mother who lived in Brussels. After Kristallnacht, there was an announcement that Belgium was taking 1,000 Jewish children and Holland was taking 1,000 Jewish children and Great Britain was taking 2,000 Jewish children. They had to be under the age of 16. My father tried to get me in [the *Kindertransport*] because we had connections, we had family there. They accepted me."[225]

Av Perlmutter left Austria in January 1939, a few weeks after the events of Kristallnacht. "My uncle, the rabbi, apparently had some contacts with the outside world and he managed to get my aunt in Holland to organize requests for my sister and myself to leave Austria as refugees to Holland. So we were fortunate enough to be part of another group of children to leave Austria. It's a little bit emotional. And the reason is that was the last time I saw my mother. It's difficult to talk about it. They took us to the train station."[226]

Sophie Nussbaum learned her father had been sent from her hometown of Emden, a seaport on the river Ems in northwestern Germany, to a concentration camp. "After a few weeks, they let the men out of the concentration camp, but now they had to work for the Gestapo, cleaning the streets. We saw lawyers and scholars out in the cold, with no hats, repairing the roads—it was a terrible sight. My mother told me it was not important what your work was as long as it did not harm another person. I was getting an education: I saw my uncles working very hard all day long, and still not earn enough money to feed their families. My father helped them a lot. We still had our shop, but now we were allowed to sell to Jewish people only between five and six o'clock in the evening.

"Then, on a certain date, we had to close the shop. My parents had to leave our house and move all six of us—grandmother too— into one room in the house of three Jewish old maids who lived on another street.

"After Kristallnacht, the Dutch government began giving visas to German and Austrian children who had relatives in Holland. Ruth and I had an aunt there who applied for us. When our visas arrived a few months later, we immediately packed up, and went with our mother by train to the border. My father stayed at home because only one parent was allowed to accompany the children.

"I'll never forget how she said goodbye, crying. Everything was terrible. My mother told me I was responsible for my sister, who was ten years old. She walked with us to the border; we said goodbye and walked across—it was only a few meters. It was January 25, 1939. I never saw my parents again."[227]

Despite all the restrictions, 120,000 German and 140,000 Austrian Jews managed to escape after Kristallnacht and before the outbreak of the war. Unfortunately, another 175,000 Jews were not so lucky. These immigration totals were also paltry given the magnitude of the problem and the danger the Jews faced in Europe.

The international reaction also reinforced Hitler's view that the world would not care what happened to the Jews. As historian Joseph Tenenbaum observed, "It is doubtful if without the demonstrable failure of Evian on July 6–13, and the Munich betrayal of September 29–30, the Nazis would have dared to stage the 'Crystal Night' pogrom of November 9–10."[228]

CHAPTER 9

The Road to Hell

While many people would feign ignorance years later about what happened during the Holocaust, claiming they were unaware of the atrocities committed by the Germans against the Jews, the events of November 9–10 were known around the world. The *New York Times* ran a story on the front page on November 11 describing the pogrom, which had not yet been given the moniker of Kristallnacht: "A wave of destruction, looting, and incendiarism unparalleled in Germany since the Thirty Years War [1618–1648] and in Europe generally since the Bolshevist Revolution swept over Great Germany today as National Socialist cohorts took vengeance on Jewish shops, offices and synagogues for the murder by a young Polish Jew of Ernst vom Rath, third secretary of the German Embassy in Paris."

The Berlin correspondent of the London *Daily Telegraph* reported on November 11:

> *Mob law ruled in Berlin throughout the afternoon and evening and hordes of hooligans indulged in an orgy of destruction. I have seen several anti-Jewish outbreaks in Germany during the last five years, but never anything as nauseating as this. Racial hatred and hysteria seemed to have taken complete hold of other-*

wise decent people. I saw fashionably dressed women clapping their hands and screaming with glee, while respectable, middle-class mothers held up their babies to see the "fun."[229]

Newspaper headlines in British and American newspapers highlighted the violence in Germany: "Anti-Jew Riots Raging" (*Evening News*, November 10); "Vienna Synagogues Blown up" (*The Times*, November 11); "Bombs Used to Set Synagogues on Fire" (*Daily Herald*, November 11); "All Vienna's Synagogues Attacked . . . " (*New York Times*, November 11).[230]

Frederick Oechsner was an American reporter in Berlin who witnessed the violence and was horrified by the damage. He was also shocked that amid all the shattered glass, there was not a lot of shouting or other noise. Eerily, he said, "It was as quiet as an execution."[231]

According to historian Deborah Lipstadt, "In the weeks following Kristallnacht, close to 1,000 different editorials were published on the topic. . . . For over three weeks following the outbreak, eyewitness reports from Germany could be found on the front pages of numerous papers. Practically no American newspaper, irrespective of size, circulation, location, or political inclination failed to condemn Germany. Now even those that, prior to Kristallnacht, had been reluctant to admit that 'violent persecution is a permanent fixture in Nazism' criticized Germany."[232]

The anti-Semitic rabble-rouser, Father Charles Coughlin, was one of the few public figures in America who was not outraged by Kristallnacht. He called it "a self-defense mechanism" against Jewish-sponsored Communism.[233]

The press was almost universally critical and not taken in by the Nazi propaganda about the spontaneity of the violence. Few papers made a connection, however, between the violence and the blatant Nazi anti-Semitism. Instead, Lipstadt notes, journalists believed the primary motivation behind the pogrom was the desire to extort money from the Jews to boost the German economy. In addition, while the Nazi threat became more widely accepted, and some reporters even began to anticipate that the plight of the Jews would worsen, the media barons of the time did not demand changes in U.S. policy. "In fact, they cautioned against them because the most efficacious and speedy solution would have necessitated ignoring two prevailing American sentiments: the necessity to maintain strict neutrality and even stricter bars to increased immigration."[234]

Besides the public media reports, diplomats based in Germany and Austria also informed their governments about the mayhem that took place on Kristallnacht. David Buffum was the U.S. consul in Leipzig. He informed his superiors that the SA not only smashed and looted property, but also attacked Jewish men, women, and children. "In one of the Jewish sections, an eighteen-year-old boy was hurled from a three-story window to land with both legs broken on a street littered with burning beds and other household furniture and effects from his family's and other apartments." Buffum visited the commercial center of the city and found that "one of the largest clothing stores in the heart of the city was destroyed by flames from incendiary bombs, only the charred walls and gutted roof having been left standing." He added that the owners of the store were charged with setting the fire, dragged from their beds at 6:00 a.m., and thrown in jail. Buffum also went to the zoo where he saw Nazis throwing Jews into the stream that ran through the park.[235]

The British consul general in Frankfurt, Robert Smallbones, reported that violence erupted at 6:00 a.m. in Wiesbaden. He said more than 2,000 Jews were arrested, all the synagogues were burned, and that the SA and SS "visited every Jewish shop and office, destroying the windows, goods, equipment."[236] Smallbones's counterpart in Hamburg witnessed similar destruction. At one point he said that "some sixty schoolchildren stoned the glass doors of a synagogue over the head of a policeman in the presence of some two hundred people."[237]

After the pogrom, Goebbels told a group of foreign correspondents why he had not ordered the police to prevent the violence. "I could not order our policemen to shoot at Germans," he said, "because inwardly I sympathized with them."[238]

✡ The Sounds of Silence ✡

No German organizations condemned the events of Kristallnacht. A few local clerics did speak out, and some were punished for doing so. Pastor Julius von Jan, for example, told his congregation in Swabia, "Houses of worship, sacred to others, have been burned down with impunity— men who have loyally served our nation and conscientiously done their duty have been thrown into concentration camps simply because they belong to a different race. Our nation's infamy is bound to bring about Divine punishment." For his forthrightness, Jan was beaten and his home vandalized. He was ultimately imprisoned.[239]

Only one prominent German prelate, Bernhard Lichtenberg, rector of Saint Hedwig's Cathedral in Berlin, had the courage to condemn the outrages publicly. Cardinal Eugenio Pacelli (future Pope Pius XII), the Vatican's secretary of state, was given a detailed report by the papal nuncio in Berlin, but the Vatican had no official reaction.

Prior to Kristallnacht, in one of his last public appearances, on October 21, 1938, Pope Pius XI condemned Hitler, likening him to Julian the Apostate (Roman Emperor Flavius Claudius Julianus), who attempted to "saddle the Christians with responsibility for the persecution he had unleashed against them."[240] Pius considered breaking relations with Hitler's Germany but was dissuaded from doing so by Pacelli, who believed instead in living in peace with Germany.[241] Pius XI died before taking any action.

The subsequent actions of Pacelli as Pope during the Holocaust have been a matter of great controversy, with Jews and many scholars believing his muted reaction following Kristallnacht was typical of his silence throughout the Holocaust and may have contributed to the catastrophe. One question Jews have asked is whether the Vatican archives reveal internal discussions among Vatican officials, including Pacelli, about the appropriate reaction to this pogrom.

While leaders in the West were quick to condemn the violence of Kristallnacht, they were reluctant to take any punitive measures against Germany. Though Britain was more responsive than most countries in terms of accepting Jewish refugees, Neville Chamberlain was not sympathetic to the plight of German Jewry. In a private letter written July 30, 1939, the British prime minister said of Kristallnacht: "I believe the persecution arose out of two motives; A desire to rob the Jews of their money and a jealousy [sic] of their superior cleverness. . . . No doubt Jews aren't a loveable people; I don't care about them myself—but that is not sufficient to explain the Pogrom."[242]

Unlike Pope Pius XII or Chamberlain, Franklin Roosevelt is generally revered for his policies before, during, and after the war, but historians have questioned his behavior during this period as well.[243] He made no immediate comment after Kristallnacht and referred questions about it to the State Department. It was only after five days of widespread public outrage that he took any action. He recalled the U.S. ambassador from Germany and held a press conference in which he proclaimed, "The news of the past few days from Germany has deeply shocked public opinion in the U.S. Such news from any part of the world would inevitably produce a similar profound reaction among American people in every part of the nation. I myself could scarcely believe that such things could happen in a 20th century civilization."[244]

Roosevelt agreed to allow 15,000 German Jews who were already in the United States to remain, but he resisted all calls to increase the overall quota of immigrants from the Nazi-occupied countries. Equally significant, his failure to take any action against Germany, or to mobilize an international coalition to challenge Hitler, sent the message that the world would not intervene to save the Jews. How much he could have done given the mood of the American public is debatable, but the consequences of his doing nothing were demonstrably catastrophic.

Beyond some brief protestations, the world took no steps to punish Germany for its treatment of the Jews on Kristallnacht. Still, the Germans learned from the outcry that future measures against the Jews should be taken beyond public view to ensure there would be no criticism or interference. Thus, when the Final Solution was ultimately formalized at the Wannsee Conference in 1942, the Nazis made every effort to disguise and conceal their actions, and the pogrom of November 9–10 was never repeated.

In the immediate aftermath of Kristallnacht, however, the Nazis boasted of their actions. The Nazi Party paper, *Völkischer Beobachter*, for example, wrote about the destruction of three synagogues in Berlin and described the scene on November 11: "All over the west side of Berlin, as in other parts of the capital where Jews still swagger and strut, not a single storefront window of a Jewish business has remained intact. The anger and fury of the citizens of Berlin, who maintained the greatest discipline despite everything, was kept within definite limits, so that excesses were avoided and not a single hair was touched on a Jewish head. The goods on display in the store windows, some of which were decorated in a quite magnificent manner, remained untouched. At the most, a few objects here and there may have been damaged as the result of a stone being hurled into a window or a fragment of glass falling."[245]

Just as the propaganda ministry had dictated to the German media how the assassination attempt on vom Rath should be covered, it also used the media to try to influence world opinion toward the pogrom. On November 11 the ministry offered the following guidelines of how and what should be reported:

> *Windows have been smashed here and there, synagogues caught fire themselves or went up in flames somehow or other. The reports should not be presented in too prominent a manner, no headlines on the first page. For the time being, there should be no photographs. Survey reports on the Reich should not be assembled, but it can be mentioned that similar actions were carried out elsewhere in the Reich. Descriptions of specific incidents in this connection should be avoided. All this should appear only on*

page 2 or 3. If editorial commentary is deemed necessary, it should be brief and state, for example, that the great and understandable popular anger provided a spontaneous answer to the murder of the third secretary.[246]

Kristallnacht was unique, even for the Nazi persecution of the Jews that came before and after. "It was the only occasion during the Third Reich," historian Ian Kershaw observed, "when the German public was confronted directly, on a nation-wide scale, with the full savagery of the attack on the Jews. Never before and never again did the persecution of the Jews stand at the forefront of the public's attention as on the morning of the 10th November 1938, when the results of what Goebbels called the 'spontaneous answer' of the German people to the murder of vom Rath were there for all to see."[247] As a member of the Hitler Youth explained, "After Kristallnacht, no German old enough to walk could ever plead ignorance of the persecution of the Jews, and no Jews could harbor any delusion that Hitler wanted Germany anything but *judenrein*, clean of Jews."[248]

Average Germans had a variety of reactions to Kristallnacht. Some found it troubling to see the brutality of their fellow Germans, and those critical of the regime, especially, worried that it might eventually be turned against them. Other Germans were offended by the destruction of property and the lawlessness and disorder that violated the norms of their orderly society. Those who believed the Nazi propaganda about the omnipotence of the Jews feared retribution. The visibility of the pogrom may have shocked and disturbed many ordinary Germans, but it also had another important effect, namely, intimidation. The ruthlessness, combined with the cold-blooded efficiency and universality of the Nazi terror "consolidated the notion in the population that all resistance was useless against the unrestrained National Socialist power."[249]

The violence officially ended on November 10, but it continued for several days in some towns and cities. One of the first places the violence stopped was Munich, where Hitler was staying at the time. He undoubtedly heard the commotion as the SA went about its business, and fire and police cars raced through the streets. After 2:00 a.m., he sent for the Munich police chief, Friedrich Karl von Eberstein, and told him to restore order. Hitler ordered other members of his staff to put a stop to looting and arson. By the time most residents woke up for school or work the next morning, the violence had come to an end.[250]

Few Jews had any doubt that Kristallnacht had been a well-organized attack on their community with the objective of scaring and humiliating them, and ultimately provoking them to leave Germany and Austria. "If it happened in one place, it was a drunken brawl," Frederick Firnbacher observed, "since it was all over, you knew it was orchestrated."[251]

The Jews' suspicions were correct; the attacks on them were premeditated, as Julius Streicher, the Nazi publisher of the anti-Semitic *Der Stürmer* newspaper, acknowledged in a memo written on April 14, 1939: "The anti-Jewish action of November 1938 did not arise spontaneously from the people. . . . Part of the Party formation have been charged with the execution of the anti-Jewish action."[252]

Interestingly, as is the case with the Final Solution, no written order exists indicating that Hitler had authorized the attacks on Kristallnacht, nor did he speak about it. This may have been a way for him to maintain deniability, but it is evident that his subordinates either received orders to seize Jewish assets and arrest Jewish males or sought his authorization. Moreover, as would often be the case in the coming year, Hitler's name would be used to silence any criticism. For example, when the Prussian minister of finance, Johannes Popitz, complained about the violence, and called on Göring to punish the perpetrators, Göring replied, "My dear Popitz, do you want to punish the Führer?"[253]

After the war, often during war crimes trials, former Nazis claimed that either they did not have any knowledge of what was going on or that they had taken measures to stop the violence. At Nuremberg, for example, von Eberstein, who, in addition to being the police chief in Munich, was SS Obergruppen-führer and chief of the SS Oberabschnitt South, testified extensively on the events of Kristallnacht. On November 9, von Eberstein said he accompanied Hitler to the meeting of the "old fighters" in the old city hall. Shortly after hearing that vom Rath had died, Hitler drove to his apartment. Von Eberstein accompanied him and was responsible for blocking traffic on the Odeon Platz. "Every year, on the night of 9 to 10 November, a meeting was held there and new recruits were sworn into the Waffen-SS. When I came to the Odeon Platz, it was reported to me that a synagogue was burning and that the firemen were being interfered with. Shortly thereafter I received a telephone call from the Chief Magistrate (Landrat) of Munich who told me that Planegg Castle on the Munich city limits, which belonged to the Jewish Baron Hirsch, had been set afire by unknown persons. The constabulary asked for assistance. This was about 11:45 p.m. At midnight Hitler came to the swearing-in ceremony. Since I could not leave my post, I sent the next highest SS leader, Brigadeführer Diehm, to the synagogue to establish order there. Besides that, I sent a police raiding squad under an officer to Planegg in order to ascertain the perpetrators and put out the fire."

Von Eberstein added, "Goebbels had made a wild speech attacking the Jews. As a result of this, considerable excesses had occurred in the city. I immediately drove through the city in a car in order to survey the situation. I saw shop windows which had been smashed; a few stores were burning. First, I immediately intervened myself and then threw all the available police on the streets with instructions to protect Jewish business establishments until further notice. In addition to that, in cooperation with one of the municipal offices of Munich, I saw to it that the shop windows were boarded up to prevent thefts and so forth. . . . I can only say that the SS, just like the Party, was anti-Semitic, but quite apart from any material loss, we considered this indecent and the SS did not participate in it."[254]

SA Obergruppenführer Max Juttner claimed during the Nuremberg trial that whenever SA men were guilty of excesses, they were punished. In fact, 14 SA men were found guilty by the Nazi Party Court of killing Jews on Kristallnacht, but they were all let off. Only three people were punished in the end for committing rape and theft. The prosecutor said a document from the regular court indicated they were released because they fell "within the line of Party comrades who, motivated by the decent National Socialist attitude and initiative, had overshot the mark."[255]

✡ The Aftermath ✡

Life for the Jews who remained in Germany and Austria changed dramatically after the pogrom. "As a result of Kristallnacht, a whole range of laws rained down on Jews that made life totally different," recalled Robert Behr. "We were no longer to go to a movie or visit an entertainment facility. Everything was off limits. There was a square with an ice cream parlor nearby where all the Jewish boys and girls used to congregate and that suddenly had a big sign that said Jews were no longer wanted. We were no longer allowed to sit on park benches unless they were painted yellow. It was something my mother and I never expected would happen. We didn't think it would happen to us. . . .

For the first time, we became scared and began to fear for our lives and didn't trust anyone. . . . We lived in a house where people had been friendly. The association that ran our building did a survey of the Christian people and they no longer would live with Jews and said we had to move out. Another letter said the caretaker of the building does no longer wish to perform his services for the Jews. He used to clean the stairs and things. This is a man we used to give a big Christmas bonus. We used to help him out and give him clothes because he had a boy my age.

You were an outcast. All the dreams we had of being part of the German people. There was nothing left that made you think you could possibly still be a German. Sure you spoke German and read German books. I remember talking to my mother for hours saying, how is it possible that a family like ours that has had the desire to be

German, and contributed to German life and culture, and fight and, if necessary, die for Germany could be so persecuted that the people did not want anything no matter what sacrifices we made? Little did we know what was to follow."[256]

"I think the bottom line," observed Geoffrey Fritzler of Breslau, "was to make it so unpleasant for anyone who wasn't carted off they would seek any ways and means to get out of the country. Basically it was an arm-twisting move to get everybody the hell out."[257]

A series of decrees were quickly issued to make the victims responsible for their own misfortune. For example, on November 12 the Executive Order Pertaining to the Restoration of the Appearance of Streets in Respect of Jewish Business Premises stated: "All damage sustained by Jewish business premises and homes in consequence of public indignation at international Jewry's campaign against National Socialist Germany will at once be made good by Jewish householders and trades people."

Paradoxically, some officials, such as Göring, were furious about the damage because the glass used in Germany came from Belgium and it became necessary to spend part of the country's foreign currency reserves to buy new glass. Even with the Jews' money it was impossible to replace all the material because the vandals had destroyed in one night the equivalent of half the Belgium glass industry's annual output.[258]

Jews as a whole were fined one billion Reichsmarks. They were excluded from all businesses, and claims against insurance companies for their burned properties were rejected. Jews were subsequently banned from any places of entertainment, such as theaters and dance halls, forbidden from enrolling in universities, and banned from German schools. All Jews were further ordered to surrender all their jewelry and other items made of gold, silver, or containing precious stones, or face imprisonment for up to 10 years.

New draconian laws and orders were subsequently issued to complete the process of Aryanization, to eliminate all Jewish institutions, to encourage Jewish emigration, and to isolate the remaining Jews from the general population. Germans saw less and less of Jews, who were always an unpopular minority, and undoubtedly grew increasingly indifferent to their fate. As Robert Kempner observed, "They were deprived of their occupations, robbed of their property, forbidden to inherit or bequeath, forbidden to sit on park benches or keep canaries, forbidden to use public transportation, forbidden to frequent restaurants, concerts, theaters, and movie houses. They were subject to specific racial laws, stripped of all their civil rights, denied freedom of movement. Their human rights and human dignity were trampled in the dust until they were deported to concentration camps and consigned to the gas chambers."[259]

Jews were frantic to get out of the Reich, but many had the more immediate worry of daily survival. Women were suddenly responsible for their families as virtually all of their husbands had been arrested on Kristallnacht. They desperately tried to find their husbands and other male family members and then get them released from prisons and concentration camps. Historian Marion Kaplan observed that women typically had different experiences than men on Kristallnacht. Some women were humiliated, beaten, or even killed, but most were not physically harmed. Instead, they were usually forced to stand by and watch as their older sons and husbands were brutalized, arrested, and taken away to an uncertain fate. Kaplan said that many memoirs mention the unforgettable scene of flying feathers. "As in Russian pogroms at the turn of the century, the mobs tore up feather blankets and pillows, shaking them into the rooms, out the windows, and down the stairways. Jews were deprived of their bedding and the physical and psychological sense of well-being it represented. Broken glass in public and strewn feathers in private spelled the end of Jewish security in Germany."[260]

Many Jews were left homeless and penniless. Many shops would not sell even basic necessities to them. As one reporter observed in Munich, Jews were "cowering from every lighted corner . . . searching for food. Every shop in this fourth biggest city in Germany today bears the inscription, 'NO JEW ADMITTED.' Food stores, cafes and restaurants, pharmacists, fruiterers and banks—in all of them hangs the same sign. And the Jews may buy their bread, their milk, only after nightfall, at back doors—if they happen to know a friendly shopkeeper."[261]

Jewish institutions were all closed, so Jews initially had no one to turn to for help. By February 1939 the Germans had created an organization to coordinate emigration, education, and social welfare for the Jews. They called it the *Reichsvertretung der Juden in Deutschland* (Federal Representation of the Jews in Germany), which was similar to an organization the Jews had set up in 1933. The new agency was kept under constant surveillance by the police.[262]

By the time the war started in September 1939, most Jews, about 370,000, had escaped Germany and Austria. The 175,000 who remained were viewed by the Nazis as hostages in case the Jews outside Germany were considering any vengeful acts. The SS newspaper declared, "Woe to the Jews if another of them, or a helper employed or incited by them, should raise his hand against a German."[263]

A few weeks after Kristallnacht, Hitler made explicit his plan for the Jews. He told the Czech foreign minister on January 21, 1939,

"We are going to destroy the Jews. They are not going to get away with what they did on November 9, 1938. The day of reckoning has come." Nine days later, Hitler publicly declared war on the Jews in a speech to the Reichstag on the anniversary of his attainment of power: "If international finance Jewry within Europe and abroad should succeed once more in plunging the peoples into a world war, then the consequence will be not the Bolshevization of the world and therewith a victory of Jewry, but on the contrary, the destruction of the Jewish race in Europe."[264]

✡ Conclusion ✡

The impact of *Kristallnacht* should not be underestimated. This was the beginning of the end for German Jewry and telegraphed the fate of all Jews who would come under Nazi control. The Nazis recognized this immediately. Foreign Minister Joachim von Ribbentrop wrote on January 25, 1939, that it was impossible to solve the emigration problem and that it was necessary to develop a radical solution to the Jewish question. He added, "It is probably no coincidence that 1938, the year of destiny, has not only brought the realization of the concept of Greater Germany, but at the same time has also brought the Jewish question close to solution."[265]

The deportation of German Jews to their deaths began in October 1941. At the end of April 1943, 150 Jewish children who had been living on a farm training to be Zionist pioneers were deported in one of the final transports of German Jews. Most died in concentration camps. Fewer than 10,000 of the 131,800 German Jews targeted for extermination by the Nazis survived. Approximately 5,000 survived by hiding, many with the help of courageous non-Jews. Another 4,700 were Jews who were saved from deportation when 3,000 of their non-Jewish wives protested their arrest in February 1943. Goebbels subsequently canceled the order and declared them "privileged persons."[266] Of the 43,700 Austrian Jews who had failed to escape the Nazis, fewer than 2,000 returned to their homes after the war.

Some people believe the Holocaust proved there was no God. After all, how could a just and loving God allow such a thing to happen? Paradoxically, a person of faith may find a divine hand in Kristallnacht because more than 200,000 Jews who probably would have never left their homes and, therefore, would have likely gone up the chimneys of Auschwitz, instead were provoked to flee to safety.

Many Germans on Kristallnacht foresaw the consequences of their countrymen's actions. "We Germans will pay dearly for what was done to the Jews last night," a German soldier's aunt told him. "Our churches, our houses, and our stores will be destroyed. You can be sure of that."[267] She was prescient. The flames of the synagogues reached up to the heavens that later brought retribution in the form of the Allied bombs that crushed the Reich.

Appendix A
Heinrich Müller's Orders to All Gestapo Offices

Transmitted at 11:55 p.m. November 9, 1938

1) Actions against Jews, especially against their synagogues, will take place throughout the Reich shortly. They are not to be interfered with; however, liaison is to be effected with the Ordnungspolizei to ensure that looting and other significant excesses are suppressed.

2) So far as important archive material exists in synagogues this is to be secured by immediate measures.

3) Preparations are to be made for the arrest of about 20,000 to 30,000 Jews in the Reich. Above all well-to-do Jews are to be selected. Detailed instructions will follow in the course of this night.

4) Should Jews in possession of weapons be encountered in the course of the action, the sharpest measures are to be taken. Verfugungstruppen der SS as well as general SS can be enlisted for all actions. Control of the actions is to be secured in every case through the Gestapo. Looting, larceny etc. is to be prevented in all cases. For securing material, contact is to be established immediately with the responsible SD . . . leadership. Addendum for Stapo Cologne: In the Cologne synagogue there is especially important material. This is to be secured by the quickest measures in conjunction with SD.[268]

Appendix B
Heydrich's Instructions for Kristallnacht

November 10, 1938
Secret
Copy of Most Urgent telegram from Munich, of November 10, 1938,
1:20 A.M.
To
All Headquarters and Stations of the State Police
All districts and Sub-districts of the SD
Urgent! For immediate attention of Chief or his deputy!
Re: Measures against Jews tonight

Following the attempt on the life of Secretary of the Legation vom
Rath in Paris, demonstrations against the Jews are to be expected in
all parts of the Reich in the course of the coming night, November
9/10, 1938. The instructions below are to be applied in dealing with
these events:

1. The Chiefs of the State Police, or their deputies, must
immediately upon receipt of this telegram contact, by telephone,
the political leaders in their areas—Gauleiter or Kreisleiter—who
have jurisdiction in their districts and arrange a joint meeting
with the inspector or commander of the Order Police to discuss
the arrangements for the demonstrations. At these discussions
the political leaders will be informed that the German Police has
received instructions, detailed below, from the Reichsführer SS and
the Chief of the German Police, with which the political leadership
is requested to coordinate its own measures:

a) Only such measures are to be taken as do not endanger German lives or property (i.e., synagogues are to be burned down only where there is no danger of fire in neighboring buildings).

b) Places of business and apartments belonging to Jews may be destroyed but not looted. The police is instructed to supervise the observance of this order and to arrest looters.

c) In commercial streets particular care is to be taken that non-Jewish businesses are completely protected against damage.

d) Foreign citizens—even if they are Jews—are not to be molested.

2. On the assumption that the guidelines detailed under para. 1 are observed, the demonstrations are not to be prevented by the Police, which is only to supervise the observance of the guidelines.

3. On receipt of this telegram Police will seize all archives to be found in all synagogues and offices of the Jewish communities so as to prevent their destruction during the demonstrations. This refers only to material of historical value, not to contemporary tax records, etc. The archives are to be handed over to the locally responsible officers of the SD.

4. The control of the measures of the Security Police concerning the demonstrations against the Jews is vested in the organs of the State Police, unless inspectors of the Security Police have given their own instructions. Officials of the Criminal Police, members of the SD, of the Reserves and the SS in general may be used to carry out the measures taken by the Security Police.

5. As soon as the course of events during the night permits the release of the officials required, as many Jews in all districts—

especially the rich—as can be accommodated in existing prisons are to be arrested. For the time being only healthy male Jews, who are not too old, are to be detained. After the detentions have been carried out the appropriate concentration camps are to be contacted immediately for the prompt accommodation of the Jews in the camps. Special care is to be taken that the Jews arrested in accordance with these instructions are not ill-treated. . . .

signed Heydrich,
SS Gruppenführer [269]

Appendix C
Estimated Number of Jews Killed in the Final Solution

Country	Estimated Pre-Final Solution Population	Estimated Jewish Population Annihilated	Percent
Poland	3,300,000	3,000,000	90
Baltic Countries	253,000	228,000	90
Germany/Austria	240,000	210,000	88
Protectorate of Bohemia and Moravia	90,000	80,000	89
Slovakia	90,000	75,000	83
Greece	70,000	54,000	77
The Netherlands	140,000	105,000	75
Hungary	650,000	450,000	70
SSR White Russia	375,000	245,000	65
SSR Ukraine*	1,500,000	900,000	60
Belgium	65,000	40,000	60
Yugoslavia	43,000	26,000	60
Romania	600,000	300,000	50
Norway	1,800	900	50
France	350,000	90,000	26
Bulgaria	64,000	14,000	22
Italy	40,000	8,000	20
Luxembourg	5,000	1,000	20
Russia (RSFSR)*	975,000	107,000	11
Denmark	8,000	--	--

*The Germans did not occupy all the territory of this republic.[270]

Appendix D
Partial List of Towns in Which Synagogues Were Destroyed

Aachen	Hechingen	Potsdam
Altdorf	Heidelberg	Quackenbrack
Aschaffenburg	Heilbronn	Regensburg
Bad Homburg	Hochburg	Rüdesheim
Baden-Baden	Hoengen	Saarbrücken
Baisingen	Hüttenbach	Saarlautern
Bamberg	Kanigsbach	Saarwillingen
Bayreuth	Kassel	Salzburg
Beckum	Kehl	Schmieheim
Berlin	Kippenheim	Siegen
Bobenhausen	Königsberg	Stettin
Brandenburg	Konstanz	Stuttgart
Bremen	Korbach	Thalfang
Breslau	Krefeld	Treuchtlingen
Broddorf	Laupheim	Tübingen
Cologne	Leipzig	Vienna
Cottbus	Mainz	Weisweiler
Dillingen	Mannheim	Wiesbaden
Dusseldorf	Marktbreit-on-Main	Wiesloch
Eberswalde	Memel	Wittlich
Eisenstadt	Merzig	Worms
Emmerich	Munich	Wuppertal
Eschwege	Nentershausen	Zeven
Essen	Ober-Ramstadt	
Giessen	Offenburg	
Hamburg	Pforzheim	

Appendix E
Jewish Emigration from the Greater Reich (including Austria and Czechoslovakia)[271]

Great Britain	40,000
France	30,000
The Netherlands	20,000
Belgium	15,000
Switzerland	8,000
Scandinavia	5,000
Poland and other Eastern European countries	30,000
Other countries in Europe	5,000
United States	60,000
Palestine	55,000
South Africa	4,500
South America	30,000
Central America	5,000
Australia	4,500
Asia (mostly Shanghai)	12,000
Other countries in overseas destinations	5,000
Total	329,000

Appendix F
Shoah Foundation Testimonies

Mitchell Bard gratefully acknowledges the USC Shoah Foundation Institute for Visual History and Education, University of Southern California, for allowing us to use the following testimonies:

Harry Alexander
Inge Angst
Hugo Beckerman
Robert Behr
Fritzi Bellamy
Eva Bergmann
Inge Berner
Gerda Bikales
Eva Brewster
Siegfried Buchwalter
Henry Cohen
Werner Cohen
Herman Cohn
Frank Correl
Joel Darmstadter
Robert Dratwa
Lucille Eichengreen
Henry Eisner
Frederick Firnbacher
Arnold Fleischmann
Erna Florsheim
Lisleotte Foster
Eric Friedmann

Geoffrey Fritzler
Gabriele Gatzert
Esther Gever
George Ginsburg
Henry Glaser
Leo Glueckselig
Gisela Golombek
Sigi Hart
Marga Hauptman
Charles Heimler
Therese Gertrude Isenberg
George Jackson
Kurt Jacoby
Fred Katz
Harry Katz
Sabina (Feuer) Katz
Alfred Kleeman
Ingrid Komar
Ernest Kopstein
Lisbeth Kornreich
Fred Kort
Henry Warner Laurant
Alexander Lebenstein

Kurt Maier
Fred Marcus
Ernest Marx
Gary Matzdorff
Robert Meier
Sol Messinger
Lothar Molton
Johanna Neumann
Peter Ney
Jill Pauly
Av Perlmutter
Leo Rechter
Edith Reisfeld
Helga Relation
Stephanie Robertson
Jutta Rose
Lore Rosen
Edmund Rosenblum
Ursula Rosenfeld
Harry Spector
Dorrit St. John
Dennis Urstein

Notes

1. Anthony Read and David Fisher, *Kristallnacht: The Unleashing of the Holocaust,* NY: Peter Bedrick Books, 1989, p. 69.

2. Gerald Schwab, *The Day the Holocaust Began,* NY: Praeger, 1990, p. 32.

3. Martin Gilbert, *The Holocaust,* NY: Henry Holt and Company, 1985, p. 183

4. Ben Austin, "Kristallnacht," in Mitchell G. Bard, ed., *The Complete History of the Holocaust,* San Diego: Greenhaven Press, 2001, p. 68.

5. Simon Wiesenthal Center, "Kristallnacht Eyewitness Accounts and Reminiscences," Speech delivered in Cologne Synagogue 9 November 1978, http://motlc.wiesenthal.com/site/ pp.asp?c=gvKVLcMVIuG&b=394831.

6. The Gestapo hired vom Rath's father in 1940 with the expectation he would be particularly antagonistic toward the Jews. Instead, at least one witness said that he actually secretly helped Jews. Robert Beir and Brian Josepher, *Roosevelt and the Holocaust*, NJ: Barricade Books, 2006, p. 125.

7. Read and Fisher, *Kristallnacht*, p. 8.

8. Bella Gutterman and Avner Shalev, eds., *To Bear Witness. Holocaust Remembrances at Yad Vashem*, Jerusalem: Yad Vashem, 2005, p. 57. Grynzspan was not the first Jew to shoot a Nazi. In 1936, David Frankfurter murdered the leader of the Swiss Nazi Party, Wilhelm Gustloff, and Hitler considered but ultimately rejected the idea of imposing a fine or otherwise collectively punishing the Jews. He probably did so because of the upcoming Berlin Olympics (Peter Loewenberg,

Notes

"The Kristallnacht as a Public Degradation Ritual," The Leo Baeck
Institute Yearbook, XXXII, London: Secker and Warburg, 1987, p. 309).
Herschel eventually came under the control of the Nazis, but he was
never brought to trial and no one knows what happened to him. He was
thought to still be alive late in the war, but was legally declared dead in
1960. His parents survived and settled in Israel where Herschel's father
testified at the trial of Adolf Eichmann (Wikipedia and *Memories of
Kristallnacht—More Than Broken Glass*, Ergo Media, A Living Memorial
to the Holocaust-Museum of Jewish Heritage, 1988).

9. Read and Fisher, *Kristallnacht*, p. 58.

10. Quoted in Benz, "The Relapse into Barbarism," in Walter H. Pehle, ed.
    November 1938 — From Kristallnacht to Genocide, NY: Berg, 1991, p. 3.

11. Lionel Kochan, *Pogrom: November 10, 1938*, Great Britain: Andre
    Deutsch Ltd., 1957, pp. 43–44.

12. Benz, "Relapse into Barbarism," pp. 3–4.

13. Saul Friedlander, *Nazi Germany and the Jews: The Years of Persecution,
    1933—1939*, (Vol. 1), NY: HarperCollins, 1997, p. 272.

14. Read and Fisher, *Kristallnacht*, p. 62.

15. Martin Gilbert, *Kristallnacht: Prelude to Destruction*, NY: Henry Holt,
    2007, p. 29.

16. Lucy Dawidowicz, *War Against the Jews, 1933–1945*. NY: Bantam
    Books, 1975, p. 101. Himmler did not like the plans for Kristallnacht
    and dictated a statement that night indicating he had been surprised
    when he learned about them and that he believed they were a result of
    Goebbels's "hunger for power and blockheaded stupidity." Similarly,
    Heydrich had long preferred to pressure the Jews to emigrate through

arrests and legal measures to economically isolate them (Stefan Kley, "Hitler and Pogrom of November 9–10, 1938," *Yad Vashem Studies* 28 (2000), p. 92).

17. Read and Fisher, *Kristallnacht*, p. 66.

18. Read and Fisher, *Kristallnacht*, p. 91.

19. Ingeborg Hecht, *Invisible Walls*, San Diego: Harcourt Brace Jovanovich, 1984, p. 58.

20. Read and Fisher, *Kristallnacht*, p. 64.

21. K.Y. Ball-Kaduri, "The Central Jewish Organizations in Berlin," *Yad Vashem Studies* 3 (1959), p. 278.

22. Benz, "Relapse into Barbarism," pp. 6–7.

23. Read and Fisher, *Kristallnacht*, p. 69.

24. Gisela Golombek, interview by Shoah Foundation Institute for Visual History and Education, University of Southern California.

25. Robert Dratwa, interview by Shoah Foundation Institute for Visual History and Education, University of Southern California.

26. Fred Marcus, interview by Shoah Foundation Institute for Visual History and Education, University of Southern California.

27. Helga Relation, interview by Shoah Foundation Institute for Visual History and Education, University of Southern California.

28. Robert Behr, interview by Shoah Foundation Institute for Visual History and Education, University of Southern California.

Notes

29. Kurt Jacoby, interview by Shoah Foundation Institute for Visual History and Education, University of Southern California.

30. Yitzhak S. Herz, "Kristallnacht at the Dinslaken Orphanage," *Yad Vashem Studies* 11 (1976), pp. 346–48.

31. Quoted in Benz, "Relapse into Barbarism," p. 23.

32. Ellen Land-Weber, *To Save a Life: Stories of Holocaust Rescue,* 2005, "Sophie Yaari Tells Her Story," http://www.humboldt.edu/~rescuers/book/Pinkhof/yaari/sophie2.html.

33. Leo Rechter, interview by Shoah Foundation Institute for Visual History and Education, University of Southern California.

34. Dennis Urstein, interview by Shoah Foundation Institute for Visual History and Education, University of Southern California.

35. Edmund Rosenblum, interview by Shoah Foundation Institute for Visual History and Education, University of Southern California.

36. Dorrit St. John, interview by Shoah Foundation Institute for Visual History and Education, University of Southern California.

37. Monroe Dodd, ed., *From the Heart: Life Before and After the Holocaust: A Mosaic of Memories,* Kansas City: Kansas City Star Books, 2001, p. 106.

38. Previously on the Web site of Cohen Center for Holocaust Studies, Keene State College.

39. Werner Cohen, interview by Shoah Foundation Institute for Visual History and Education, University of Southern California.

40. Henry Cohen, interview by Shoah Foundation Institute for Visual History and Education, University of Southern California.

41. Frank Correl, interview by Shoah Foundation Institute for Visual History and Education, University of Southern California.

42. Lucille Eichengreen, interview by Shoah Foundation Institute for Visual History and Education, University of Southern California.

43. Therese Gertrude Isenberg, interview by Shoah Foundation Institute for Visual History and Education, University of Southern California.

44. Kurt Maier, interview by Shoah Foundation Institute for Visual History and Education, University of Southern California.

45. The Panel of Time Witnesses, http://timewitnesses.org/english/~susan.html.

46. Lothar Molton, interview by Shoah Foundation Institute for Visual History and Education, University of Southern California.

47. Gilbert, *Kristallnacht*, p. 61.

48. Alexander Lebenstein, interview by Shoah Foundation Institute for Visual History and Education, University of Southern California.

49. Inge Angst, interview by Shoah Foundation Institute for Visual History and Education, University of Southern California.

50. Lore Rosen, interview by Shoah Foundation Institute for Visual History and Education, University of Southern California.

51. Peter Ney, interview by Shoah Foundation Institute for Visual History and Education, University of Southern California.

Notes

52. Fred Katz, interview by Shoah Foundation Institute for Visual History and Education, University of Southern California.

53. Previously on the Web site of Cohen Center for Holocaust Studies, Keene State College.

54. Jill Pauly, interview by Shoah Foundation Institute for Visual History and Education, University of Southern California.

55. Ingrid Komar, interview by Shoah Foundation Institute for Visual History and Education, University of Southern California.

56. Harry Spector, interview by Shoah Foundation Institute for Visual History and Education, University of Southern California.

57. Harry Alexander, interview by Shoah Foundation Institute for Visual History and Education, University of Southern California.

58. U.S. Holocaust Memorial Museum (cited hereafter as USHMM), interview with Carola Steinhardt, June 3, 1996, http://collections.ushmm.org/artifact/image/h00/00/h0000261.pdf, p. 7.

59. Previously on the Web site of Cohen Center for Holocaust Studies, Keene State College.

60. Read and Fisher, *Kristallnacht*, pp. 92–93.

61. Marga Hauptman, interview by Shoah Foundation Institute for Visual History and Education, University of Southern California.

62. Sigi Hart, interview by Shoah Foundation Institute for Visual History and Education, University of Southern California.

63. Ernest Marx, interview by Shoah Foundation Institute for Visual History and Education, University of Southern California.

64. Hugo Beckerman, interview by Shoah Foundation Institute for Visual History and Education, University of Southern California.

65. Frederick Firnbacher, interview by Shoah Foundation Institute for Visual History and Education, University of Southern California.

66. Arnold Fleischmann, interview by Shoah Foundation Institute for Visual History and Education, University of Southern California.

67. Henry Glaser, interview by Shoah Foundation Institute for Visual History and Education, University of Southern California.

68. Bryan Mark Rigg, *Hitler's Jewish Soldiers*, Lawrence: University of Kansas Press, 2002, p. 72. On his 85th birthday in 1932, German President Paul von Hindenburg was presented with a book listing all the Jews who had died in World War I.

69. Arnold Fleischmann, interview by Shoah Foundation Institute for Visual History and Education, University of Southern California.

70. Alexander Lebenstein, interview by Shoah Foundation Institute for Visual History and Education, University of Southern California.

71. Herz, "Kristallnacht at the Dinslaken Orphanage," p. 349.

72. Gilbert, *Kristallnacht*, pp. 48–49.

73. Alfred Kleeman, interview by Shoah Foundation Institute for Visual History and Education, University of Southern California.

74. Gilbert, *Kristallnacht*, p. 57.

75. Ernest Kopstein, interview by Shoah Foundation Institute for Visual History and Education, University of Southern California.

76. Esther Gever, interview by Shoah Foundation Institute for Visual History and Education, University of Southern California.

77. George Jackson, interview by Shoah Foundation Institute for Visual History and Education, University of Southern California.

78. Charles Heimler, interview by Shoah Foundation Institute for Visual History and Education, University of Southern California.

79. Leo Glueckselig, interview by Shoah Foundation Institute for Visual History and Education, University of Southern California.

80. Fritzi Bellamy, interview by Shoah Foundation Institute for Visual History and Education, University of Southern California.

81. Harry Katz, interview by Shoah Foundation Institute for Visual History and Education, University of Southern California.

82. Henry Warner Laurant, interview by Shoah Foundation Institute for Visual History and Education, University of Southern California.

83. Gilbert, *Kristallnacht*, p. 43.

84. Herman Cohn, interview by Shoah Foundation Institute for Visual History and Education, University of Southern California.

85. Joel Darmstadter, interview by Shoah Foundation Institute for Visual History and Education, University of Southern California.

86. Lisleotte Foster, interview by Shoah Foundation Institute for Visual History and Education, University of Southern California.

87. Eric Friedmann, interview by Shoah Foundation Institute for Visual History and Education, University of Southern California.

88. Gabriele Gatzert, interview by Shoah Foundation Institute for Visual History and Education, University of Southern California.

89. Av Perlmutter, interview by Shoah Foundation Institute for Visual History and Education, University of Southern California.

90. Sabina (Feuer) Katz, interview by Shoah Foundation Institute for Visual History and Education, University of Southern California.

91. Stephanie Robertson, interview by Shoah Foundation Institute for Visual History and Education, University of Southern California.

92. Jutta Rose, interview by Shoah Foundation Institute for Visual History and Education, University of Southern California.

93. USHMM, interview with Armin Kern, RG-02.182, I Remember Germany, [microform] 1993.

94. USHMM, interview with Kurt Ladner, Kristal Night, RG-02.192, Not a Moment to Soon [microform].

95. Quoted in Joshua M. Greene and Shiva Kumar, *Witness: Voices from the Holocaust,* New York: Touchstone, 2000, pp. 27–28.

96. Hannele Zürndorfer, *The Ninth of November,* London: Quartet Books, 1989, pp. 60–64.

97. Johanna Neumann, interview by Shoah Foundation Institute for Visual History and Education, University of Southern California.

98. Mark Jonathan Harris and Deborah Oppenheimer, *Into the Arms of Strangers: Stories of the Kindertransport*, NY: Bloomsbury, 2000, pp. 74–75.

99. Mark M. Anderson, ed., *Hitler's Exiles*, NY: New Press, 1998, pp. 71–72.

Notes

100. Monika Richarz, ed. *Jewish Life in Germany, Memoirs from Three Centuries*, Bloomington: Indiana University Press, 1991 pp. 390–91, quoted in *"But the Story Didn't End That Way..."* Yad Vashem, 2000, p. 45–46.

101. Fred Marcus, interview by Shoah Foundation Institute for Visual History and Education, University of Southern California.

102. Benz, "Relapse into Barbarism," p. 30.

103. Harris and Oppenheimer, *Into the Arms of Strangers*, p. 57.

104. Lisbeth Kornreich, interview by Shoah Foundation Institute for Visual History and Education, University of Southern California.

105. Fred Kort, interview by Shoah Foundation Institute for Visual History and Education, University of Southern California.

106. Alfred Kleeman, interview by Shoah Foundation Institute for Visual History and Education, University of Southern California.

107. USHMM, interview with Ernest Heppner, May 10, 1989, http:// collections.ushmm.org/artifact/image/h00/00/h0000088.pdf, p. 6.

108. USHMM, interview with Kurt Klein, March 13, 1992, Scottsdale, AZ.

109. Simon Wiesenthal Center, Museum of Tolerance, "A Personal Memoir by Michael Bruce," http://motlc.wiesenthal.com/site/ pp.asp?c=gvKVLcMVIuG&b=394831.

110. Shlomo Samson, *Between Darkness and Light: 60 Years after "Kristallnacht,"* Jerusalem: Rubin Mass Ltd. 1998, p. 48.

111. Selma Schiratzki, "The Rykestrasse School—A Jewish Elementary School during the Hitler Period in Berlin," *Year Book of the Leo Baeck Institute*, 5, London: East End Library, 1960, p. 305.

112. Quoted in Kochan, *Pogrom*, pp. 72–73.

113. Inge Berner, interview by Shoah Foundation Institute for Visual History and Education, University of Southern California.

114. USHMM, interview with Gad Beck, February 16, 1996, http://collections.ushmm.org/artifact/image/h00/00/h0000049.pdf, p. 8.

115. Read and Fisher, *Kristallnacht*, pp. 70–72.

116. Gilbert, *Kristallnacht*, p. 112.

117. Benz, "Relapse into Barbarism," pp. 12–13.

118. Henry Eisner, interview by Shoah Foundation Institute for Visual History and Education, University of Southern California.

119. Robert Meier, interview by Shoah Foundation Institute for Visual History and Education, University of Southern California.

120. USHMM, interview with Jacob Wiener, June 30, 1994, http://collections.ushmm.org/artifact/image/h00/00/h0000203.pdf, pp. 9–11.

121. Gary Matzdorff, interview by Shoah Foundation Institute for Visual History and Education, University of Southern California.

122. USHMM, interview with Anna Bluethe (born Becker), Anna and Leo Bluethe letters Concerning Kristallnacht in Kaiserslautern, Germany, 1939, RG-02.099 [microform].

Notes

123. Gilbert, *Kristallnacht,* pp. 133–34.

124. Nuremberg Trial Proceedings, Vol. 2, Second Day, Wednesday, 21 November 1945.

125. Kochan, *Pogrom,* p. 66.

126. Gilbert, *Kristallnacht,* p. 94.

127. Gilbert, *Kristallnacht,* p. 35.

128. Benz, "Relapse into Barbarism," p. 16.

129. Benz, "Relapse into Barbarism," p. 17.

130. Ernest Günter Fontheim, "Personal Memoir of Kristallnacht," haGalil Online, http://www.hagalil.com/deutschland/berlin/gemeinde/fontheim .htm.

131. Rita Thalman and Emmanuel Feinermann, *Crystal Night, 9–10 November 1938,* NY Holocaust Library, 1972, p. 64.

132. *Year Book of the Leo Baeck Institute,* 5 London: East End Library, 1960, p. 305.

133. Ernest Günter Fontheim, Personal Memoir of Kristallnacht, http://www. hagalil.com/deutschland/berlin/gemeinde/fontheim.htm.

134. George Ginsburg, interview by Shoah Foundation Institute for Visual History and Education, University of Southern California.

135. Eva Bergmann, interview by Shoah Foundation Institute for Visual History and Education, University of Southern California.

136. Inge Berner, interview by Shoah Foundation Institute for Visual History and Education, University of Southern California.

137. Eva Brewster, interview by Shoah Foundation Institute for Visual History and Education, University of Southern California.

138. Harris and Oppenheimer, *Into the Arms of Strangers*, pp. 65–66.

139. Quoted in Jonathan C. Friedman, *The Lion and the Star—Gentile-Jewish Relations in Three Hessian Communities*, KY: University Press of Kentucky, 1998, p. 157.

140. Gilbert, *Kristallnacht*, pp. 97–98.

141. Gerda Bikales, interview by Shoah Foundation Institute for Visual History and Education, University of Southern California.

142. Siegfried Buchwalter, interview by Shoah Foundation Institute for Visual History and Education, University of Southern California.

143. Gilbert, *Kristallnacht*, p. 33.

144. Gilbert, *Kristallnacht*, p. 33.

145. Arnold Fleischmann, interview by Shoah Foundation Institute for Visual History and Education, University of Southern California.

146. Erna Florsheim, interview by Shoah Foundation Institute for Visual History and Education, University of Southern California.

147. Gilbert, *Holocaust*, pp. 72–73.

148. Sol Messinger, interview by Shoah Foundation Institute for Visual History and Education, University of Southern California.

Notes

149. Alfred Kleeman, interview by Shoah Foundation Institute for Visual History and Education, University of Southern California.

150. Ursula Rosenfeld, interview by Shoah Foundation Institute for Visual History and Education, University of Southern California.

151. USHMM, interview of Peter Becker by Jean Brock, September 26, 1991, RG50.166.004.

152. "Kristallnacht in Baden-Baden, Germany," Yad Vashem, http://yad-vashem.org.il/exhibitions/from_our_photo_archive/data/kristallnacht/home_kristallnach.html.

153. Simon Wiesenthal Center, Museum of Tolerance, "A Letter by a Firefighter," http://motlc.wiesenthal.com/site/pp.asp?c=gvKVLcMVIuG&b=394831.

154. Previously on the Web site of Cohen Center for Holocaust Studies, Keene State College.

155. Quoted in Beir and Josepher, *Roosevelt and the Holocaust*, p. 126.

156. Quoted in Read and Fisher, *Kristallnacht*, p. 84.

157. Quoted in Read and Fisher, *Kristallnacht*, pp. 106–7.

158. Gilbert, *Kristallnacht*, pp. 92–93.

159. Gilbert, *Kristallnacht*, pp. 117–18.

160. Quoted in *"But the Story Didn't End That Way,"* Yad Vashem, pp. 42–43.

161. Quoted in Friedlander, *Nazi Germany and the Jews*, p. 278.

162. Henry Oertelt, *An Unbroken Chain—My Journey Through the Nazi Holocaust*, Minneapolis: Lerner Publications, 2000, pp. 19–20.

163. Quoted in Franziska Becker and Utz Jeggle, "Memory and Violence: Local Recollections of Jewish Persecution during the *Reichskristallnacht*," *Yad Vashem Studies*, 20, 1990, p. 102.

164. Quoted in Kochan, *Pogrom*, pp. 74–75.

165. Benz, "Relapse into Barbarism," pp. 10–12.

166. Read and Fisher, *Kristallnacht*, p. 75.

167. Benz, "Relapse into Barbarism," p. 14.

168. *Year Book of the Leo Baeck Institute*, 15, London: East and West Library, 1970, p. 167.

169. Eva Fogelman, *Conscience and Courage*, NY: Anchor Books, 1994, p. 27.

170. Gilbert, *Kristallnacht*, p. 52.

171. Read and Fisher, *Kristallnacht*, pp. 105–6.

172. Inge Berner, interview by Shoah Foundation Institute for Visual History and Education, University of Southern California.

173. Siegfried Buchwalter, interview by Shoah Foundation Institute for Visual History and Education, University of Southern California.

174. Frank Correl, interview by Shoah Foundation Institute for Visual History and Education, University of Southern California.

175. Read and Fisher, *Kristallnacht*, p. 93.

Notes

176. Gilbert, *Kristallnacht*, pp. 43–44.

177. Gilbert, *Kristallnacht*, p. 57.

178. Gilbert, *Kristallnacht*, p. 76.

179. Richard Fuchs, "The Hochschule under Nazi Rule," *Year Book of the Leo Baeck Institute*, 12, 1967, p. 25.

180. Gilbert, *Kristallnacht*, pp. 84–85.

181. Gilbert, *Kristallnacht*, p. 86.

182. Read and Fisher, *Kristallnacht*, p. 73.

183. Gilbert, *Kristallnacht*, p. 95.

184. Quoted in Marion A. Kaplan, *Between Dignity and Despair*, NY: Oxford University Press. 1998, p. 124.

185. Edith Reisfeld, interview by Shoah Foundation Institute for Visual History and Education, University of Southern California.

186. Bernt, Engelmann, *In Hitler's Germany*, NY: Pantheon. 1986, pp. 130–37.

187. Read and Fisher, *Kristallnacht*, pp. 97–98.

188. Friedlander, *Nazi Germany and the Jews*, p. 276.

189. Quoted in *"But the Story Didn't End That Way,"* Yad Vashem, p. 43. See also Friedlander, *Nazi Germany and the Jews*, pp. 269–70.

190. Friedlander, *Nazi Germany and the Jews*, pp. 274–75.

191. Benz, "Relapse into Barbarism," p. 13.

192. Read and Fisher, *Kristallnacht,* p. 101.

193. Gilbert, *Kristallnacht,* p. 30.

194. Gilbert, *Kristallnacht,* p. 37.

195. "Kristallnacht," Yad Vashem, http://www1.yadvashem.org/exhibitions/kristallnacht/home_kristallnacht.html.

196. "Kristallnacht," Yad Vashem, http://www1.yadvashem.org/exhibitions/kristallnacht/home_kristallnacht.html.

197. "Kristallnacht," Yad Vashem, http://www1.yadvashem.org/exhibitions/kristallnacht/home_kristallnacht.html.

198. "Kristallnacht," Yad Vashem, http://www1.yadvashem.org/exhibitions/kristallnacht/home_kristallnacht.html.

199. Read and Fisher, *Kristallnacht,* p. 80.

200. "Kristallnacht," Yad Vashem, http://www1.yadvashem.org/exhibitions/kristallnacht/home_kristallnacht.html

201. *Year Book of the Leo Baeck Institute,* 15, London: East and West Library, 1970, p. 167.

202. Read and Fisher, *Kristallnacht,* pp. 94, 96.

203. Read and Fisher, *Kristallnacht,* pp. 102–3.

204. Gilbert, *Kristallnacht,* pp. 71–72.

Notes

205. Read and Fisher, *Kristallnacht*, p. 101.

206. Thalman and Feinermann, *Crystal Night*, p. 70.

207. USHMM, interview with Martha Bauer, April 30, 1992, RG50.166.003.

208. "Kristallnacht," Yad Vashem, http://www1.yadvashem.org/exhibitions/kristallnacht/home_kristallnacht.html.

209. "Kristallnacht," Yad Vashem, http://www1.yadvashem.org/exhibitions/kristallnacht/home_kristallnacht.html.

210. Read and Fisher, *Kristallnacht*, p. 109; Gilbert, *Kristallnacht*, p. 69.

211. Friedlander, *Nazi Germany and the Jews*, p. 276.

212. Kaplan, *Between Dignity and Despair*, p. 181.

213. Herz, "Kristallnacht at the Dinslaken Orphanage," p. 361.

214. *Memories of Kristallnacht—More Than Broken Glass*, Ergo Media, A Living Memorial to the Holocaust-Museum of Jewish Heritage, 1988.

215. Leni Yahil, *The Holocaust: The Fate of the European Jewry, 1932–1945*, NY: Oxford University Press, 1987, p. 118.

216. Ball-Kaduri, "Central Jewish Organizations in Berlin," p. 280.

217. Mitchell G. Bard, *Forgotten Victims: The Abandonment of Americans in Hitler's Camps*, Boulder, CO: Westview Press, 1994, p. 10.

218. "The United States and the Refugee Crisis," Supplementary Reading Materials, United States Holocaust Memorial Museum,

http://www.ushmm.org/museum/exhibit/online/stlouis/teach/supread.htm
Gilbert, *Kristallnacht*, pp. 212–13.

219. Frank Correl, interview by Shoah Foundation Institute for Visual History and Education, University of Southern California.

220. *Memories of Kristallnacht—More Than Broken Glass*, Ergo Media, A Living Memorial to the Holocaust-Museum of Jewish Heritage, 1988.

221. Alfred Kleeman, interview by Shoah Foundation Institute for Visual History and Education, University of Southern California.

222. Interview with Edward Adler, Wentworth Films, Inc.; Holocaust, February 27, 1992.

223. Fritzi Bellamy, interview by Shoah Foundation Institute for Visual History and Education, University of Southern California.

224. Read and Fisher, *Kristallnacht*, p. 72.

225. George Ginsburg, interview by Shoah Foundation Institute for Visual History and Education, University of Southern California.

226. Av Perlmutter, interview by Shoah Foundation Institute for Visual History and Education, University of Southern California.

227. Ellen Land-Weber, *To Save a Life: Stories of Holocaust Rescue*, 2005, "Sophie Yaari Tells Her Story," http://www.humboldt.edu/~rescuers/book/Pinkhof/yaari/sophie2.html.

228. Joseph Tenenbaum, "The Crucial Year 1938," *Yad Vashem Studies* 2 (1958), pp. 49–50.

229. Read and Fisher, *Kristallnacht,* p. 68.

230. Gilbert, *Kristallnacht,* pp. 58–59.

231. *Memories of Kristallnacht—More Than Broken Glass*, Ergo Media, A Living Memorial to the Holocaust-Museum of Jewish Heritage, 1988.

232. Deborah Lipstadt, *Beyond Belief,* NY: Free Press, 1993, p. 99.

233. Beir and Josepher, *Roosevelt and the Holocaust,* p. 126.

234. Lipstadt, *Beyond Belief,* pp. 110–11.

235. Read and Fisher, *Kristallnacht,* p. 84.

236. Gilbert, *Kristallnacht,* p. 34.

237. Gilbert, *Kristallnacht,* p. 75.

238. Gilbert, *Kristallnacht,* p. 40.

239. Gilbert, *The Holocaust,* p. 73.

240. Archbishop Amleto Cicognani, apostolic delegate to the United States, certainly informed the Vatican of the public broadcast of the American bishops' condemnation of Kristallnacht. Rychlak, A Response to The Vatican and the Holocaust: A Preliminary Report by the International Catholic-Jewish Historical Commission, Catholic League, (11/2000), at http://www.catholicleague.org/rer.php?topic==The+Church+and+the+Holocaust&id=62.

241. Beir and Josepher, *Roosevelt and the Holocaust,* p. 127.

242. Gilbert, *Kristallnacht,* p. 222.

243. See, for example, David S. Wyman, *The Abandonment of the Jews: America and the Holocaust, 1941–1945*, NY: New Press, 1998, and Bard, *Forgotten Victims*.

244. Beir and Josepher, *Roosevelt and the Holocaust*, p. 127.

245. Benz, "Relapse into Barbarism," pp. 18–19.

246. Benz, "Relapse into Barbarism," p. 15.

247. Ian Kershaw, "Persecution and German Popular Opinion," *Year Book of the Leo Baeck Institute*, 15, London: Secker and Warburg, 1981, p. 275.

248. Daniel Jonah Goldhagen, *Hitler's Willing Executioners: Ordinary Germans and the Holocaust*. NY: Knopf, 1996, p. 102.

249. Kershaw, "Persecution and German Popular Opinion," p. 280.

250. Read and Fisher, *Kristallnacht*, p. 98.

251. Frederick Firnbacher, interview by Shoah Foundation Institute for Visual History and Education, University of Southern California.

252. Nuremberg Trial Proceedings Volume 2, Second Day, Wednesday, 21 November 1945.

253. Friedlander, *Nazi Germany and the Jews*, p. 279.

254. Nuremberg Trial Proceedings, Volume 20: One Hundred and Ninety-Fourth Day, Saturday; 3 August 1946.

255. Nuremberg Trial Proceedings Volume 21: Two Hundred and Fourth Day, Thursday; 15 August 1946.

256. Robert Behr, interview by Shoah Foundation Institute for Visual History and Education, University of Southern California.

257. Geoffrey Fritzler, interview by Shoah Foundation Institute for Visual History and Education, University of Southern California.

258. Benz, "Relapse into Barbarism," p. 20.

259. Quoted in Hecht, *Invisible Walls*, p. 57.

260. Kaplan, *Between Dignity and Despair*, p. 125.

261. Gilbert, *Kristallnacht*, p. 146.

262. Dawidowicz, *The War Against the Jews*, p. 105.

263. Gilbert, *Kristallnacht*, pp. 153–54.

264. Dawidowicz, *The War Against the Jews*, p. 106.

265. Tenenbaum, "The Crucial Year 1938," p. 50.

266. Gilbert, *Kristallnacht*, pp. 262–65.

267. Engelmann, *In Hitler's Germany*, p. 139.

268. The History Place, "World War Two in Europe," http://www.historyplace.com/worldwar2/timeline/knacht1a.htm.

269. Nuremberg Documents PS-3051.

270. *Holocaust Denial: A Pocket Guide*. Anti-Defamation League, 1997.

271. *"But the Story Didn't End that Way."*

Bibliography

Anderson, Mark M., ed. *Hitler's Exiles*. New York: New Press, 1998.

Anti-Defamation League. *Holocaust Denial: A Pocket Guide*. New York: Anti-Defamation League, 1997.

Austin, Ben. "Kristallnacht," in *The Complete History of the Holocaust*, edited by Mitchell G. Bard. San Diego: Greenhaven Press, 2001, pp. 65–69.

Ball-Kaduri, K. Y. "The Central Jewish Organizations in Berlin," *Yad Vashem Studies* 3 (1959).

Bard, Mitchell G., ed. *The Complete History of the Holocaust*. San Diego: Greenhaven Press, 2001.

———. *Forgotten Victims: The Abandonment of Americans in Hitler's Camps*. Boulder, CO: Westview Press, 1994.

Becker, Franziska, and Utz Jeggle, "Memory and Violence: Local Recollections of Jewish Persecution during the *Reichskristallnacht*," *Yad Vashem Studies* 20 (1990): pp. 99–114.

Beir, Robert, and Brian Josepher. *Roosevelt and the Holocaust*. Fort Lee, NJ: Barricade Books, 2006.

Benz, Wolfgang. "The Relapse into Barbarism." In *November 1938: From Kristallnacht to Genocide*, edited by Walter H. Pehle. New York: Berg, 1991, pp. 1–43.

Berenbaum, Michael, ed. *Witness to the Holocaust*. New York: HarperCollins, 1997.

Dawidowicz, Lucy S. *The War Against the Jews, 1933–1945*. New York: Bantam, 1975.

Dodd, Monroe, ed. *From the Heart: Life Before and After the Holocaust: A Mosaic of Memories*. Kansas City: Kansas City Star Books, 2001.

Engelmann, Bernt. *In Hitler's Germany*. New York: Pantheon, 1986.

Eschwege, Helmut, "Resistance of German Jews against the Nazi Regime," Publications of the Leo Baeck Institute, Year Book, XV, London: East and West Library, 1970: 143–82.

Fogelman, Eva. *Conscience and Courage*. New York: Anchor Books, 1994.

Friedlander, Saul. *Nazi Germany and the Jews: The Years of Persecution, 1933–1939*. Vol. 1. New York: HarperCollins, 1997.

Friedman, Jonathan C. *The Lion and the Star: Gentile-Jewish Relations in Three Hessian Communities*, Lexington: University Press of Kentucky, 1998.

Fuchs, Richard. "The Hochschule under Nazi Rule," *Year Book of the Leo Baeck Institute* 12 (1967): pp. 3–31.

Gilbert, Martin. *The Holocaust*. New York: Henry Holt, 1985.

———. *Kristallnacht: Prelude to Destruction*. New York: Henry Holt, 2007.

Goldhagen, Daniel Jonah. *Hitler's Willing Executioners: Ordinary Germans and the Holocaust*. New York: Knopf, 1996.

Greene, Joshua M., and Shiva Kumar. *Witness: Voices from the Holocaust*. New York: Touchstone, 2000.

Gutman, Israel, ed. *Encyclopedia of the Holocaust*. Vol 1. New York: Macmillan, 1990, pp. 836–40.

Gutterman, Bella, and Avner Shalev, eds. *To Bear Witness: Holocaust Remembrances at Yad Vashem*. Jerusalem: Yad Vashem, 2005.

Harris, Mark Jonathan, and Deborah Oppenheimer. *Into the Arms of Strangers: Stories of the Kindertransport*. New York: Bloomsbury, 2000.

Hecht, Ingeborg. *Invisible Walls*. San Diego: Harcourt Brace Jovanovich, 1984.

Herz, Yitzhak S. "Kristallnacht at the Dinslaken Orphanage." *Yad Vashem Studies* 11 (1976): pp. 344–68.

Hilberg, Raul. *The Destruction of the European Jews*. New York: Holmes & Meier, 1985.

Kaplan, Marion A. *Between Dignity and Despair*. New York: Oxford University Press, 1998.

Kershaw, Ian. "Persecution and German Popular Opinion," *Year Book of the Leo Baeck Institute* 26 (1981): pp. 261–98.

Kley, Stefan. "Hitler and the Pogrom of November 9–10, 1938." *Yad Vashem Studies* 28 (2000): pp. 87–112.

Kochan, Lionel. *Pogrom: November 10, 1938*. London, UK: Andre Deutsch, 1957.

Lipstadt, Deborah. *Beyond Belief*. New York: Free Press, 1993.

Loewenberg, Peter. "The Kristallnacht as a Public Degradation Ritual," *Year Book of the Leo Baeck Institute* 32 (1987): pp. 309–23.

More Than Broken Glass: *Memories of Kristallnacht*, VHS. Produced, directed, and written by Chris Pelzer. Teaneck, NJ: Ergo Media, 1989.

Nuremberg Trial Proceedings, Vol. 2, Second Day. Wednesday, 21 November 1945; Vol. 20, One Hundred and Ninety-Fourth Day. Saturday, 3 August 1946; Vol. 21, Two Hundred and Fourth Day. Thursday, 15 August 1946. (Trial of the Major War Criminals Before the International Military Tribunal, Nuremberg, 14 November 1945–1 October 1946.)

Oertelt, Henry. *An Unbroken Chain: My Journey Through the Nazi Holocaust*. Minneapolis: Lerner Publications, 2000.

Read, Anthony, and David Fisher. *Kristallnacht: The Unleashing of the Holocaust*. New York: Peter Bedrick, 1989.

Richarz, Monika, ed. *Jewish Life in Germany: Memoirs from Three Centuries*. Bloomington: Indiana University Press, 1991.

Rigg, Bryan Mark. *Hitler's Jewish Soldiers*, Lawrence: University of Kansas Press, 2002.

Samson, Shlomo. *Between Darkness and Light: 60 Years after "Kristallnacht."* Jerusalem: Rubin Mass, 1998.

Schiratzki, Selma. "The Rykestrasse School—A Jewish Elementary School during the Hitler Period in Berlin," *Year Book of the Leo Baeck Institute* 5 (1960): pp. 299–307.

Schwab, Gerald. *The Day the Holocaust Began.* New York: Praeger, 1990.

Shirer, William. *The Rise and Fall of the Third Reich: A History of Nazi Germany.* New York: Fawcett, 1991.

Speer, Albert. *Inside the Third Reich.* New York: Touchstone, 1997.

Tenenbaum, Joseph. "The Crucial Year 1938," *Yad Vashem Studies* 2 (1958): pp. 49–77.

Thalman, Rita, and Emmanuel Feinermann, *Crystal Night, 9–10 November 1938.* Translated by Gilles Cremonesi. NY: Holocaust Library, 1972.

Wistrich, Robert S. *Who's Who in Nazi Germany.* New York: Routledge, 1995.

Wyman, David S. *The Abandonment of the Jews: America and the Holocaust, 1941–1945.* New York: New Press, 1998.

Yad Vashem. *"But the Story Didn't End That Way . . ."* Jerusalem: Yad Vashem International School for Holocaust Studies, 2000.

Yahil, Leni. *The Holocaust: The Fate of the European Jewry, 1932–1945.* New York: Oxford University Press, 1987.

Zürndorfer, Hannele. *The Ninth of November.* London: Quartet Books, 1989.

Index

Index

About the Author

Mitchell Bard is the executive director of the nonprofit American-Israeli Cooperative Enterprise (AICE) and one of the leading authorities on U.S.-Middle East policy. Dr. Bard is also the director of the Jewish Virtual Library (http://www.Jewish VirtualLibrary.org), the world's most comprehensive online encyclopedia of Jewish history and culture. For three years he was the editor of the *Near East Report*, the American Israel Public Affairs Committee's (AIPAC) weekly newsletter on U.S. Middle East policy. Dr. Bard has appeared on the BBC, Fox News, al-Jazeera, MSNBC, NBC, CBC, the *Jenny Jones Show*, and other local and national television and radio outlets. His work has been published in academic journals, magazines, and major newspapers. He has written and edited nineteen books. Bard holds a doctoral degree in political science from the University of California, Los Angeles, and a master's degree in public policy from the University of California, Berkeley. He received his bachelor's degree in economics from the University of California at Santa Barbara.